CONTENTS

Introduction	
Before Call Up	10
Deenethorpe Plane Crash	13
Call Up	14
Training	18
Arriving at the hostel at Townhill	19
Visit to the Dentist	21
First Journey Underground	22
Dunfermline	23
The hostel at Newtongrange	26
Talk by a member of the French Resistance	29
Visit to the Lady Victoria	30
My first visit to Newtongrange Village	31
Meeting my room mates	34
The hostel dance	36
Working on the Pithead	36
My last days on the Pithead	39
My first day down the Lady Victoria	40
Going down on the bogies	42
Arriving at Whitehill Mine	44
The hostel dance	49
My second day at work	50
Visiting Chapelhall	55
Doing my laundry	56
Needing new clothes	57
Going dancing	57
A visit to Airdrie Palais	58
A visit to Dennison Palais	59
Bellshill dancing	60

CONTENTS continued

Meeting Robert in Airdrie 61
A visit to Armadale Hostel.. 62
My accident 62
V.E. Day Celebrations 66
Returning to Newtongrange 68
Summer holidays 70
V.J. Day 70
First Aid Training 73
Attending a road accident... 82
Meeting the Union 82
My first visit to a coal face 84
Vesting Day/Nationalisation... 86
Robert's injury 87
The roof fall 88
The day the cage dropped 90
The winter of 1946/47 93
Cosgroves 96
Visit to Cosgroves coal face 97
The accident at Cosgroves 98
The day the sole came off my boot 99
My de-mob 100
Notification of release 101
My last day as a Bevin Boy 103
Going home to Corby... 105
Starting back to work 106
Returning to Newtongrange 106
Visit to the Lady Victoria Scottish Mining Museum (2000) 108

ACKNOWLEDGEMENTS

I would like to give my grateful thanks to the following:

To my wife Lily for her patience when I disappeared for hours on end to write my story.

To Lily and the rest of my family, Joan, George, Roslynn and Grandsons Andrew, Paul and Ian for buying me a computer as a Christmas present when I was struggling to write by hand

To my Grandsons Paul and Ian for helping me with the Computer and to Paul for his drawings included in this book.

I would also like to thank Douglas Livingstone who first read my early hand written copy and encouraged me to carry on writing.

My special thanks to my daughter Joan for the many hours she spent working on the draft.

Thanks also to my brother in law John Walton and his friend Alex Smith for their assistance.

Many thanks to the Scottish Mining Museum for allowing me to use some of the photographs in this book

Special thanks to Campbell Drysdale Mining Museum photographer for allowing me to use the photographs of me taken in front of the museum and the presentation of the bench to the Bevin Boys in April 2002.

Thanks also to Ian McAlpine of C.I.S.W.O. for his support and the Midlothian Advertiser

DEDICATION

I would like to dedicate my book to my friends and workmates at the Lady Victoria who looked after me during my service as a Bevin Boy.

Also to the mining community in Newtongrange and to the many friends I made who made me feel at home. Special thanks to Lily's family who made me so welcome.

Introduction

In 1940-41 there was a shortage of miners as they were leaving the industry. They were finding employment in munitions work or joining the services. The miners were looking for work with better pay and working conditions. It soon became apparent that increased production was required and mining became a reserved occupation. The ex-miners were encouraged to return to coal mining from other industries and from the armed forces.

Despite these measures and the option to choose underground mining instead of military service or call-up, there were nowhere near enough men added to the workforce. By mid 1943, fewer than ever youngsters were enrolling as miners. Nearly half the workforce was over forty.

In July 1943 Ernest Bevin announced that every tenth man called up for National Service would be conscripted into the coalmines. On many occasions it was one in five. These young men became knows as 'Bevin Boys'. A ballot was drawn each month and it was said that his secretary would draw a number from 0-9 out of his bowler hat.

Everyone who registered for call-up during the war was given a registration number. If the last digit of the registration number was the same as the one drawn out of the hat, then that person was conscripted to work in the coalmines. Very few exceptions were allowed yet there was more resistance to call-up for the mines than for the services. Some men accepted imprisonment rather than endure the working conditions of a miner. 21,000 reluctant young men were drafted in this way. Volunteers and Optants made the number up to 42,000. In August 1944 the number taken out of Mr. Bevin's hat was a 3. My registration number was CNQ 5123. Therefore, under the ballot system I had to report for work in the mines. I became a Bevin Boy

Hostels were built to accommodate the Bevin Boys. They consisted of lines of Nissan Huts built on concrete blocks similar to an army camp. The Bevin Boys presence in the mines ensured that enough coal was produced to maintain the war effort. When the war in Europe finished in May 1945 the draw was cancelled. However, those of us who were already working in the mines had to remain there until de-mobbed in 1948. We were given a de-mob number similar to the army. The majority of Bevin Boys served 3years and 6months. I served for 3 years and 9 months before I was released in July 1948.

As one of the 21,000 Bevin Boys conscripted to work in the coalmines between

1943 and 1948 instead of the armed forces, I considered that I was more prepared than many of the other Bevin Boys for the work required in the coalmines. I was born in a mining village called Chapelhall. This village was about three miles from Airdrie and I lived there until I was 16 years old. While growing up I had heard stories about the terrible conditions that miners worked under and the serious accidents that had occurred. I must have had mining in my blood somewhere.

I decided to write about my experiences as a Bevin Boy when my grandson Paul suggested it to me. We had visited the Lady Victoria at the Scottish Mining Museum soon after it opened. On our visit Paul and I reported to what was the Main Office to join the other visitors to have a look round the Museum. The guides issued each of us with a safety helmet and two tokens before leading us across the main road towards the pit. When we reached the main gates I hesitated for a few minutes. Looking ahead I could see that everything was so familiar. My mind went back to the time when I was a Bevin Boy at this pit more than 40 years earlier.

It seemed like yesterday when on my first day I was walking through those gates with my Training Officer Mr. Tom Walton. I was looking at the stairs in front of us when Paul nudged me to tell me that the others were waiting. I followed them up the stairs to the pithead. As I looked around the pithead and at the entrance to the cage which I had travelled on so many times, the memories came flooding back. I felt so proud when I said to the guides that I had worked there for nearly four years as a Bevin Boy. The other visitors just looked at me. When we returned to the office the guides asked me lots of questions.

My story is about my time as a Bevin Boy at the Lady Victoria. It is about the terrible working conditions, the dangers and the risks. However, it is mostly about the comradeship and the many friends I made at work and in the community where I lived during this time. Without this I would not have been able to cope.

I was one of those eighteen-year-old lads from all over the United Kingdom who were conscripted and sent to work in the coalmines. They came from all walks of life. Many of them had lived in the cities and some were from the Scottish Highlands. Some had never seen a coalmine in their lives before. It must have been a terrible shock to them. Many of us were prepared and ready to do our National Service in one of the armed forces and had some idea of what to expect. We were not prepared for the type of work we had been sent to do in the coalmines

My service started at the beginning of October 1944 when I was sent to the Muircockhall Training Centre in Fife for four weeks training. From there I went to Newtongrange which is about 8 miles from Edinburgh. I was to be employed at The Lady Victoria Pit until July 1948. The Lady Victoria was one of the most modern pits in Scotland at that time and was opened by the Lothian Coal Company around the end of the 19th century.

Newtongrange was and still is a lovely village and was one of the most modern mining villages in Scotland at the time. The village was build to accommodate the families of the miners who would be working in the Lady Victoria when it opened. While working at the colliery I lived in the Miners Hostel just outside Newtongrange with 250 other Bevin Boys.

Every Bevin Boy would have his own story to tell about his experiences in the coalmines. Some would be worse than others as this would depend on the area where they worked and the conditions they worked under.

This is my story as I remember it.

Before Call Up

Seamless tube mill: tube passing through dies.
STEWARTS AND LLOYDS, LTD., GLASGOW, BIRMINGHAM, LONDON

I had moved to live in Corby in Northamptonshire from Scotland in December 1942 when I was 16 years of age. I started working at Stewarts & Lloyds and worked in the Tube Works. There we made Seamless Steel Tubes/Pipes. My job was very hot and dirty and there was a continual smell of gas from the furnaces. The noise was deafening all of the time. We didn't wear ear defenders in those days.

Like everyone else I accepted the bad conditions feeling that I was doing my bit to help the war effort. The Manager's name was Jock Reid and the Foreman was Bert Cole. None of us who worked in the Tube Mills at the time knew just how important the job was that we were working on. We only knew that it was called Project 99. We learned later that we were making pipes for PLUTO (Pipe Line under the Ocean). This was to be the means of carrying vital oil supplies from England to Normandy during the invasion of Europe.

I worked a 10 ½ hour day shift one week and 10 hours night shift the next. On night shift production would often be stopped for a time and the furnaces shut down when the siren sounded. German bombers would have crossed the coast and were nearing Corby often on their way to bomb Coventry. We wouldn't take any chances however and would make our way to the air raid shelters until the 'all clear' sounded.

A number of bombs were dropped in Corby and some damage caused to the houses around the steel works. We were very surprised that there was not more damage as the Germans had built part of Stewarts & Lloyds in Corby and knew all about its steel and tube works.

At the end of the shift I would often be leaving work at about 6.30a.m. to catch the bus home. I would stop and look in the direction of Deenethorpe and watch the planes taking off. This was one of the many American Airfields around Corby and was about 3 miles away. At that time of the morning the airfield would be lit up and I could hear the engines of the Flying Fortresses. These and other planes would then join in formation waiting for the planes from other bases nearby to join them. They would then all leave for another daylight raid on Germany. Sadly many of the men and planes did not return. On my way home from the evening shift, I would see the British Lancasters leaving on one of their many night raids over Occupied Europe.

There were many American service men in and around Corby at that time. They were very popular with the local girls and very kind to the children. They would organise parties for the children especially at Christmas time. Watching the planes taking off reminded me of the time when I first met some of the Airmen. There was a lot of excitement in Corby and in the surrounding villages when the Americans first arrived early in 1943. When the Flying Fortresses first arrived many of us would walk to the airfield to see them. We were fascinated by them and couldn't believe how big they were. We had only ever seen the planes on the cinema screens before then. From the footpath around the camp we could see the control tower which was still standing until 1996.

My younger brother Jim was about 12 years old at the time. He would often visit the Airfield along with some of his school friends. After school and at the weekends they would visit and ask for chewing gum. The favourite saying was, 'any gum chum'. They would be keen to have anything that the Yanks, as we called them, would part with. Stewarts and Lloyds Pipe Band and Highland Dancers from Corby were invited to entertain the Airmen at the airfield on a number of occasions. My father was one of the drummers.

The first time I met any of the American Airmen personally was at a weekend party. It happened when I was at a dance in the Raven Hall in Corby. At the time I was a shy 17 year old and often found it difficult to walk across the dance floor to ask a girl to dance as we did in those days. The girls were always on one side of the dance floor and we lads would stand on the opposite side.

As soon as the band struck its first note there would be a mad rush across the floor by the lads to pick one of the girls to dance with. I was often too slow. Often when I crossed the floor to choose a dancing partner she was already on the floor dancing with someone else. I always felt embarrassed having to walk back again. My mates told me to have two or three girls in mind before leaving my side of the hall. If one had gone then I could ask another.

Although we were separate in the dance hall there was often a lounge where couples could sit together and talk and perhaps have a cool drink. It was at one of these dances that I met a girl who after a few dances together, invited me to a party at her house later. We left before the dance finished and walked to her home. When we arrived her mother had made lots of sandwiches and jellies etc, much of it supplied by the Americans. There was always plenty of drink and cigarettes which they also supplied.

These luxuries were most welcome as they were always in short supply in Britain during the war years. There were about six or seven Americans there and they were not more than two or three years older than I was. They always loved to visit the homes of the local people and meet the families. Most of them had their girl friends with them at the party.

The party was well on its way when we arrived. No one introduced themselves but everyone just gave a wave of the hand and said 'hi'. We ate lots of food and those who wanted to could have plenty to drink. We played games and danced to the records that were popular at the time. The others were still there when I left in the early hours of the morning.

I went to the dance in the Raven Hall the following Saturday evening and met the same girl. I was invited to the party again that night. She left with one of her girl friends to help her mother prepare the food. Again I was made welcome and most of the others were there. Some of them had been at the party the week before.

I soon became aware that this party wasn't going as well as the previous one. There was less singing and dancing and perhaps more drinking and smoking. I then noticed that three of the young American Airmen were sitting on their own looking very upset. When I asked my friends mother what was wrong she told me that some of their friends had not returned from a mission. I didn't feel like staying at the party after that.

Later when I saw the Flying Fortresses taking off in the mornings after work I always remembered those brave young lads at the party. They were not much older than me and had lost their friends or buddies as they called them. Sadly it happened every day after each mission until the end of the war. When I was away from home and feeling a bit down I would think about those brave young men and what they were going through. It made me think that working in the pits was not so bad after all. It could be much worse.

My grandson Paul is a member of the American Airman's Historical Society and collects memorabilia of the war years. We visited what was left of the airfield on a number of occasions. Like me he was very upset when we visited there one day. We saw that the Control Tower, which had been standing there since the war years, had been demolished leaving a pile of concrete. We both felt that it should have been repaired and kept as a memorial to those brave Airmen.

For many years now American ex-servicemen have visited the Airfields, or what is left of them. They come to pay their respects to their former comrades and to visit old friends they had met while over here. There are fewer visiting each year as they are all in their late seventies or early eighties. They too were very upset when on one of their visits to Deenethorpe they saw that the Control Tower had been demolished.

Deenethorpe Plane Crash

I remember one morning at the beginning of December 1943. It was a Sunday and I was still in bed when I heard a terrific bang. I thought that there had been an accident in the Steel Works. On the Monday we learned what had happened.

We were told that a Flying Fortress with a full load of bombs had been unable to gain enough height for take off. The plane had crash-landed in the village of Deenethorpe and caught fire.

Fortunately none of the crew was injured and they were able to get out of the plane and warn the villagers. Unbelievably, some were still asleep. The quick action of the airmen prevented a tragedy and everyone was able to get clear before the plane and bombs blew up.

Call up

A few weeks before we were due to register for National Service my twin brother Robert and I went to Northampton to volunteer. We were made welcome. We had been told that anyone who volunteered would be accepted into the service of his or her choice. At the time I wanted to join the Navy. Robert's choice was the Royal Air Force.

The man who was taking down our details asked us where we worked. When we told him Stewarts & Lloyds, Corby he told us to go home as we were in a Reserved Occupation. However, a few weeks later we were called up for National Service. We had to go as did many of the young lads who worked beside us in the Tube Works. It was about May 1944 and Robert my twin and I were 17 years and 9 months old. Thinking about it afterwards, the priority work for P.L.U.T.O. must have been finished by then and the job no longer a reserved occupation.

On the morning of July 4th we had to report for our Medical Examination at Northampton. We had just come off night shift we were not feeling our best. When the medical was over Robert had passed but I was told that I had to return at a later date. My next examination date was on my birthday the 15th August. Again I had just come off night shift and was glad when my medical was over. This time I had passed.

After our medical we were all greeted by a Senior Officer of the army who was attached to one of the Scottish Regiments. He must have recognised my Scottish accent and perhaps thought here is a potential recruit. He promised me that if I signed up for 12 years he would get me into any Scottish Regiment of my choice. He also told me that if I did sign on he would make sure I would not be called up to work in the coalmines. I turned down his offer as I didn't fancy

NATIONAL SERVICE ACTS, 1939 to 1941.

GRADE CARD.

Registration No. CNQ 5123

Mr. RALSTON

whose address on his registration card is

82 Westfield Road
Derby

was medically examined on 16 AUG '44   4 JUL '44

at NORTHAMPTON MEDICAL BOARD

and placed in

GRADE* I (one)

Chairman of Board

Medical Board stamp NORTHAMPTON

Man's Signature George Ralston

*The roman numeral denoting the man's Grade (with number also spelt out) will be entered in RED ink by the Chairman himself e.g., Grade I (one) Grade II (two) (a) (Vision).

N.S. 55   [P.T.O.

DESCRIPTION OF MAN.

Date of birth 15.8.26

Height 5 ft 6 3/8 ins.

Colour of eyes Grey

Colour of hair Black

If before you are called up for service you have any serious illness or serious accident, or have reason to think there has been a deterioration in your health, you should immediately inform the Local Office of the Ministry of Labour and National Service whose address appears on the back of your registration form N.S.2, giving full particulars, including any medical evidence you can supply, and quoting your Registration No. and other entries made on form N.S.2, so that the information can be considered before an enlistment notice is issued to you.

If this Certificate is lost or mislaid, the fact must be at once reported.

The finder should send it to the nearest Local Office of the Ministry of Labour and National Service.

Wt. 51898/3084 500M 4/42 C.N.&Co.Ltd. 749 (7527)

---

serving 12 years in the army in any regiment. I thought later that perhaps he knew something about the Bevin Boys that I didn't.

I then had to return home and wait to see which service I would be joining. At the time I was looking forward to doing my National Service as Robert and most of my friends had already gone.

Prior to this time I had been in the Army Cadets for more than three years hoping to join the army. Robert had been in the A.T.C. for the same time expecting to join the R.A.F and had a number of flying hours. However, it wasn't to be. Robert was

15

> **MINISTRY OF LABOUR AND NATIONAL SERVICE**
>
> .Regional Office.
>
> 1944
>
> Dear Sir,
>
> COALMINING CALL-UP.
>
> The Government has decided that the essential man power requirements of the coalmining industry should be met by making underground coalmining employment an alternative to service in the Armed Forces and by directing to such employment a number of men who would otherwise be available for call-up for service in the Armed Forces.
>
> *Method of Selection.*—The method of selecting men for direction to this employment has been made public. It is by ballot and is strictly impartial. Your name is amongst those selected.
>
> *Training.*—Men who have had no previous experience of the coalmining industry are to be given four weeks preliminary training on both surface and underground work at special Training Centres organised by the Ministry of Labour and National Service for the purpose. Men will then be directed to working collieries for employment and will there receive (subject to special conditions in South Wales) a further fortnight's training before being employed on work below ground. Accordingly I have to notify you that it is proposed to direct you to attend in the near future at a Training Centre for a course of training with a view to subsequent employment in coalmining.
>
> *Conditions.*—The enclosed leaflet E.D.L.94 gives information about training for and employment in coalmining.
>
> *Appeals.*—You may appeal against this notification if you consider that there are any special circumstances connected with coalmining which would make it an exceptional hardship for you to be employed on that work. I have to remind you, however, that at the time of your medical examination under the National Service Acts you had an opportunity to apply for postponement of liability to be called up under these Acts. If, therefore, you appeal against this notification, your appeal should show in what way you consider that employment in coalmining would be an exceptional hardship to you having regard to the fact that either you made no application for postponement of call up or your application has been determined and postponement, if granted, has expired. If there has been any material change in your circumstances since you previously had an opportunity of applying for postponement, or renewal of postponement you should call particular attention to this fact in your appeal.
>
> If you decide to appeal, you may obtain a form on which to appeal (L.A.B.3 (C.M.D.)) from any Local Office of the Ministry of Labour and National Service, or you may appeal by letter. You should post your completed appeal *within four days* to the address
>
> E.D 608 (Revised).

notified that he had to join the army. He was very disappointed but it was nothing compared to how I felt when I was informed that I had been called up to serve as a Bevin Boy.

My Registration number ended in a 3 and as that was the number drawn out of the hat for the month of August. I was conscripted to work in the coalmines. I learned recently that the ballot numbers for the month of July were Nos.1 & 2. If I had passed my first medical on the 4th of July I would have escaped being called up as a Bevin Boy. Such is fate.

shown at the head of this letter. There will be no opportunity to appeal at a later date when you are issued with a direction to a training centre or to a working colliery.

If you make an appeal it will be put before the Local Appeal Board and the Board will make a recommendation which will be taken into account.

Unless it is decided after appeal to a Local Appeal Board that you should not be directed to coalmining employment you will be required to attend at a Training Centre.

Allocation.—Men are mainly required for coalmining employment in Durham, Lancashire, Midlands, Northumberland, Notts. and Derby, Yorkshire, Scotland and Wales.

No guarantee can be given of employment in any of these areas, but individual preferences will be taken into account as far as possible.

If you have a preference for employment in any of the areas indicated you should write (even if you make an appeal against this notification) to the address shown at the head of this letter stating your preference and stating the address of any relatives or friends in a coalmining district with whom you could live. If no statement of preference is received within a week of the date of this letter, it will be assumed that you do not wish to express any preference. It will not be possible to take account of preference which may be expressed subsequently.

On completion of training at the Training Centre you will be directed to a working colliery. Any preference for employment in a particular area which you may have expressed in reply to this notification will then be taken into account as far as possible, even if you have been required to undertake your training in another area.

Yours faithfully,

G. R. RANKIN

for Regional Controller.

Mr....

(32843) Wt. 51179—8010 50m 2/44 D.L. G. 373

I was shocked as was my father. He didn't want me to work in the coalmines as he knew the conditions that miners worked under. It didn't help me at this time when I remembered some of the stories I had heard when I was growing up. These were about the conditions the miners worked under and some of the serious accidents that had taken place around Lanarkshire where we had lived before moving to Corby.

My call up papers mentioned that I could appeal which I did. I went in front of a panel of three but needless to say I was unsuccessful. My case was that my twin brother and I had always been together and I would like to join him in the army. The panel asked me to leave the room while they made their decision. After a few minutes they called me into the room. Their suggestion was to ask my brother to join me in the coalmines. I couldn't ask him to do that. (Call-up for the coalmines was given priority over other services at that time).

Training

Bevin Boys were given a choice of which coal mining area they would prefer to work in but no guarantee of being sent there. As there were coalmines near where my grandparents lived in Lanarkshire where I grew up I chose Scotland. I was informed that I had to report to Muircockhall Training Centre on Monday 2nd October 1944. I would receive four weeks training and I would be living in the Miners' Hostel at Townhill just outside Dunfermline, Fife.

A week before I was due to leave I made the necessary arrangements with my employer Stewarts & Lloyds. I explained that I had been called up and would be finishing working there the following Friday and for them to have my wages ready before I left. Everything was ready for me to collect on the day. I went from there to the Labour Exchange to collect my travel warrant for the journey to Scotland. I handed it to the booking office clerk at Corby railway station on the Sunday and received my rail ticket for the journey.

The train left about 10pm and was due to arrive at Waverley Station in Edinburgh about 9 o'clock next morning. The journey was very unpleasant. Mostly service personnel either going on leave or returning to their camp packed the train as usual during wartime. The carriages and the corridors were full. Everyone was trying to find a space to get comfortable. People would be sitting on kit bags, cases, or even on the floor. They would be trying to get a few minutes sleep or just to take the weight off their feet. They were often disturbed at each station with passengers getting off or on the train.

Although I was on my way to do my National Service I felt self-conscious that I was not in uniform. I always felt like this when travelling during the war years. Those who were in uniform and also members of the public would wonder and sometimes ask why I was not in the services. I had nothing to show that I was doing my National Service in the coalmines.

Arriving at the hostel at Townhill

I was very tired when I arrived at Waverley Station and was looking forward to relaxing with a nice cup of tea and a sit down. It was not to be as just then an announcement came over the 'Tannoy' for all Bevin Boys to report on one of the platforms. Someone was there to meet us and to arrange the next part of our journey. We joined the train for Dunfermline and I travelled over the Forth Bridge for the first time.

I should have been excited but I was too tired. When we arrived at Dunfermline we caught the bus to the Miners' Hostel at Townhill about 2 miles away. We reported to the office, checked in and received a settling in grant of 24 shillings and sixpence, (£1.22 in today's money). This was for one weeks lodging allowance. I was then shown to my hut which I would share with another eleven lads for the next four weeks.

By the time I had unpacked had a wash and freshened up it was time for breakfast. I met the others in the dining room where we had a nice breakfast. We then met our Supervisor who took us to the Training Pit at Muircockhall. We were each issued with a Safety Helmet and Safety Boots which was our only free issue. I was upset when I had to give up six valuable clothing coupons for the boots. Before being shown round the Training Centre we were given a brief explanation of the daily programme for the next four weeks.

While the Supervisor was talking I was watching the others and wondering if they felt as nervous as I did. Were they thinking as I was how would I cope being away from home for the first time. Will I be able to mix and get on with the other lads and how dangerous will the work be? The supervisor went on to tell us that each day would be made up of physical training inside and outside. This was to get us fit for the work we would be doing down the mines. We would also be getting plenty of food to build us up. I don't think I took in all that he was saying.

Some of the training was spent in the classroom on the theory of mining. I liked that part best as it was clean and I found it interesting. With so many Bevin Boys coming and going during training it was difficult to remember names and to overcome the problem many of the lads put their name on their safety helmet. I wanted to let my mates know where I came from so I put Corby on my helmet. During my training everyone called me 'Corby '. I removed the name from my helmet before leaving Muircockhall.

After a couple of weeks training I was part of a group chosen to visit the Mining College in Cowdenbeath where we were shown many things about the Theory of Mining. My Training Officer was pleased when I told him that I found it very interesting and that I would like another visit sometime.

I got the impression that Muircockhall had not been long opened for training as some of us spent a lot of time laying kerbstones and making roads. I was given this job quite often. I had done this type of work before and was quite good at it. I learned how to do this when I was 16 years old working in the Brick Works about a mile outside Airdrie. It was my third job. I started work on my 14th birthday in a factory making ammunition boxes.

When I started work in the brickwork's my first job was helping to make a new side road into the works. I worked along with another lad about my age and we had an adult in charge of us. I learned how to line up the kerbstones and mix the cement. I was taught how to lay them in position and level them using a piece of string and spirit level. The work was heavy but I learned a lot. Although I was only a teenager at the time I was expected to do the work of an adult. There was a shortage of adults as many of them were away on their National Service. Little did I know that this experience would help me when I was training as a Bevin Boy.

It was October and I found it cold work. I couldn't afford gloves which might have helped. I also found it cold doing physical training especially as it was mostly outside and we only wore shorts and a vest. To try to keep warm we mostly played football on top of the Bing. It was familiar to me as I often played on one as a youngster when I lived in Chapelhall. They were seen in all the mining areas. The bings were made from the waste brought up from the coalmines and stacked on the surface and looked just like small hills. This one was quite flat on top but unfortunately the ball kept going over the side. We spent more time recovering the ball than we did playing football. When our grandparents were short of coal, Robert and I would join our Uncle digging for coal on the bing. We would carry it home in small bags to stock up their coal cellar for the winter months.

At the end of my first day I returned to the hostel with the others and got washed and changed. I introduced myself to my roommates and had a chat about the day's events and where each of us came from. The other Bevin Boys were from different parts of Scotland and couldn't understand why I came all the way from England to work in the pits there. I then went down to the canteen for dinner with a couple of the lads who were on their second weeks training.

Later I went to Dunfermline for a night at the pictures and to give me a chance to see the town. When we returned to the hostel I went for a cup of tea while the others went to the hut to get ready for bed. When I returned to my hut there was a bit of a commotion. Two of the lads on the opposite side of the hut from me were putting their beds together. I asked the lad in the bed next to mine what was going on. He told me that the two lads thought as it was so cold they would be warmer if they put the four blankets on top of the two beds instead of two on each. However, when the Caretaker came in he told them to put everything back as it was. It was very cold in the huts. The floor was concrete, there was no heating and we were on the East Coast of Scotland. Coming from the Midlands I probably felt the cold more than the other lads.

Visit to the Dentist

I think it was on my second day in the hostel when I woke up during the night with toothache. When I was ready for work I reported to the office and I was given some sort of powder to ease the pain. I was advised to report to my training officer to let him know as soon as I arrived at the pit. After attempting to eat something I left with some of the other lads and went to the Training Pit. I saw one of the supervisors and told him that I had toothache and asked if he knew where I could find a dentist.
He phoned one in Dunfermline and arranged an appointment for me. He gave me brief instructions to find the surgery. I caught the bus to the centre of Dunfermline and soon found it upstairs on one of the side streets. When I climbed the stairs the Dentist was waiting for me. There was no receptionist and he said go through and sit on the chair. He followed me in and after a quick look in my mouth he gave me an injection in one of my back teeth. He then left the room and then was back again to pull out my tooth. It was too soon for the anaesthetic to have taken effect.

I was holding on to the arm of the dentist's chair but it didn't help, I felt he was pulling me out of it. After a lot of pain the tooth came out and I jumped out of the chair, paid my money and ran down the stairs. I couldn't get out of the surgery quick enough. I felt a bit better when I got into the fresh air. I sat on the outside step for a few minutes until I felt a bit better before going to catch the bus back to the training pit. While I was on the bus my mouth started to go numb. The dentist hadn't given the injection enough time to take effect. When the supervisor saw me he asked what happened and when I told him he said to go for a rest and to see him later. The experience put me off dentists for a long time.

First journey underground

After a few days training on the surface it was time for some of us to venture underground. This was something I wasn't looking forward to. There were about twelve of us in the group waiting nervously to go onto the cage. We were chatting and telling jokes to try to calm us down. I remember it was a small cage and only big enough to hold about five or six of us, including the supervisor. The cage went down for the first time and I waited nervously for it to return, as I would be on the next cage going down. When it reached the top, like the others, I hesitated before stepping on, not knowing what to expect. The supervisor was on the cage waiting for us. We were a bit cramped and it was a rough journey. The runners or guides looked like pieces of flat timber about six inches wide and about an inch and a half thick. After a few minutes we reached the pit bottom.

As we made our way off the cage the supervisor told us to watch where we were walking and to mind the rails. The pit bottom wasn't as big as I thought it would be. It was perhaps about eight feet high and about the same width. The lighting wasn't bad but it felt cold and damp. We were standing with our backs to the cage waiting for the next group and were paying attention to the supervisor when the next cage arrived at the bottom. Suddenly there was a commotion behind us and we turned round to see one of the group members lying on the floor. He appeared to be having a fit of some kind. As soon as he had recovered he was taken back to the surface. I don't know what happened to him but I didn't see him again.

The supervisor who was in charge of our group took us further inside to show us how the hutches were pulled along the haulage road. He then gave us a demonstration on the method used. I shall try to describe it. The steel rope runs along the top of the hutches. A chain about 6 feet long with a hook at each end was used to pull them. The hook at one end of the chain was attached to an eye on the hutch and the other end of the chain was wound around the travelling rope 2 or 3 times. It then slipped into the other hook. When the chain gripped tight the hutches moved along. It looked very dangerous to me and I kept back as I didn't want to try it just in case I would lose any of my fingers. I don't know how long we were down the pit but it didn't seem more than an hour but it was long enough. I am pleased to say that that was the only time I was underground at the Training Pit.

The four weeks training passed much quicker than I thought it would. I quite enjoyed it, especially the friendship with my mates in the hostel and at work. Everyone wanted to help each other as we were all in the same situation. The supervisors were very helpful and didn't put us under any pressure.

Dunfermline

The hostel was only about 2 miles from Dunfermline. This was a lovely town where I spent many happy hours. I often went to the pictures and to the dancing with my mates. I also visited the Abbey. One Saturday I went to the dancing at the ice rink with another of my roommates. His name was Ian Campbell if I remember right. His parents lived in Dunfermline. I saw him a few times after I moved to Newtongrange. When we visited the ice-rink I thought we were going there to watch the ice skaters but when we arrived there was also a dance floor attached. It was at one end of the ice rink for those who preferred dancing while the ice skaters were enjoying themselves at the other end.

On the few occasions I went there was always a great band playing and the dancing was always very popular. During the interval we would watch the skaters enjoying themselves. I would find it a bit cold after a time and was pleased when the dance band started playing again. Dunfermline is a lovely town and I enjoyed the four weeks I spent there. Sadly I haven't been back since.

At the end of our training each of us was notified which pit or area we would be sent to and given a Travel Warrant. I was given a piece of paper to tell me to report to Newbattle Collieries at Newtongrange, which is about 8 miles from Edinburgh. My employer would be the Lothian Coal Company. I don't know who made the decision or how the choice was made to allocate each Bevin Boy to which Colliery. Perhaps it was just another lottery like the scheme itself and depended on the luck of the draw. If it was then this time I was lucky.

SCHEDULE

Employment in or about a coal mine

with* .... The Lothian Coal Co. Ltd., ...

at† .... Newbattle Colliery, Newtongrange. ....

under the instruction and supervision provided for in Article 2 (1) (a) (i) of the Coal Mining (Training and Medical Examination) Order, 1944, with a view to employment on work below ground

beginning on......... 30st October, ... 194 at 7 a.m.

particulars of which are as follows :—
Report at pit on Monday, 30th October, between 2.30 p.m. and 4p.m.
The rate of remuneration and conditions of service will be the agreed district rate and conditions ....

Further particulars .... Travel on Monday, 30th October by L.N.E.R. to Newtongrange. Live at Newtongrange Hostel. ....

* Insert name of Company.
† Insert name and address of Pit.
50M 5/44 CN&CoLtd 749 (2231)

I booked out of the Hostel at Townhill early on Monday October 30th 1944 and took the bus to Dunfermline railway station where I caught the train to Edinburgh. I would be travelling over the Forth Bridge for the second time which was something I was looking forward to. It seemed a short journey and the train seemed to slow down passing over the bridge. I threw a coin into the river as I was told it was lucky. I believe it worked. Once again I arrived at

MINISTRY OF LABOUR AND NATIONAL SERVICE

Emergency Powers (Defence) Acts, 1939-1940

DIRECTION ISSUED UNDER REGULATION 58A OF THE DEFENCE (GENERAL) REGULATIONS, 1939.

NOTE.—Any person failing to comply with a direction under Regulation 58A of the Defence (General) Regulations, 1939, is liable on summary conviction to imprisonment for a term not exceeding three months, or to a fine not exceeding £100 or to both such imprisonment and such fine. Any person failing to comply after such a conviction is liable on a further conviction to a fine not exceeding five pounds for every day on which the failure continues.

To Mr. George Ralston,   Govt. Training Centre,
82 W. Glebe Road,   Townhill, Dunfermline.
Corby, Nr. Kettering. (Date) 24/10/44.

In pursuance of Regulation 58A of the Defence (General) Regulations, 1939, I, the undersigned, a National Service Officer within the meaning of the said Regulations, do hereby direct you to perform the services specified by the Schedule hereto (see overleaf) being services which, in my opinion, you are capable of performing.

If you become subject to the provisions of an Essential Work Order in the employment specified in the Schedule, the direction will cease to have effect and your right to leave the employment will be determined under that Order. Otherwise, this direction continues in force until 21/4/45 or until withdrawn by a National Service Officer.

I hereby withdraw all directions previously issued to you under Regulation 58A of the said Regulations and still in force.

National Service Officer.

E.D. 383B   [P.T.O.

Waverley Station. It was very busy mostly with service personnel dashing around. After getting instructions to the bus station I made my way across Princes Street to St. Andrews Square. I had a quick look at Walter Scott's Monument and the Castle when I had crossed the road. This was my first visit to Edinburgh. It looked a beautiful City. I promised myself that I would visit again as soon as possible.

The hostel at Newtongrange

A few minutes after I arrived at St. Andrews Square a bus came in. I asked the Conductress if it was the right bus for Newtongrange and she said that it was but that I would have to change at Dalkeith Fountain and catch the Birkinside bus. This was the bus that would take me to the hostel. After about fifteen minutes the bus arrived at Dalkeith. I had only a few minutes to wait before the Birkinside bus arrived. When I got on I asked the conductress to let me off at the Miners' hostel in Newtongrange. As soon as we arrived there she called out 'Bevin Huts'! I learned later that this is what they were called locally. As I got off the bus I saw a pit in front of me. I was told later that the pit was called Lingerwood. I wondered if I might be working there. When I turned round to cross the road I saw the hostel. It was behind a stone wall about waist high.

The hostel was similar to the one I had just left except that it looked smaller. The hostel was made up of Nissan huts painted green and built on a concrete base. As I walked through the entrance the sleeping quarters for about 250 lads was on my left. There was a road on my right as I looked straight ahead and on the left hand side was the manager's bungalow. Behind this was the accommodation for the staff that lived on site. Directly opposite were four corrugated huts joined together and bricked up at the front. This was the office and the recreation part of the hostel which was made up of different rooms.

There was a quiet room for reading and writing letters, tea room and a large lounge where dances and concerts were held. The staff arranged these. Also in this building was the dining hall and kitchen. Looking directly ahead from there to the bottom of the road I saw the Sick Bay. This had five beds for

treating in-patients and also for treating minor injuries. There was a nurse in charge helped by a young assistant.

The first thing I had to do was report to the office and book in. I handed over my ration book and paid my week's lodging allowance of £1.5 shillings, (£1.25 in today's money). This covered a week's accommodation. I then received tickets for breakfast and dinner. I also had to buy tickets for sandwiches to take to work for my lunch break. I know it doesn't seem much to pay but my weekly wage was only £2.15 shillings (after deducting tax and my lodgings this left me with about £1.10 shillings (£1.50). Not much for working down the pit. I was later issued with my Hostel Membership Card. After I had booked in at the office I was shown to my sleeping quarters.

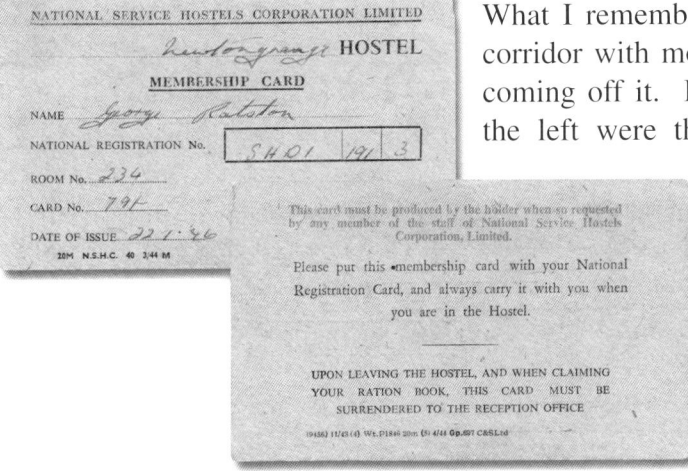

What I remember of them was a long corridor with more than a dozen doors coming off it. Inside the first door on the left were the baths and then the showers. An open doorway led to the drying room. The drying room was much higher and wider than the other huts. Within the drying room there were five or more rows of tubular structures about eight feet wide by eight feet high fixed to the floor. Pulleys were attached to these to raise and lower framed clothes holders. We called them baskets. These were used for drying wet pit clothes or drying personal laundry. We would hang our clothes over the basket and then pull the rope to raise them to the required height. We would then tie the rope to hold the basket in position until the clothes were dry. There was a separate place at the bottom of the basket for holding boots or shoes if they were wet. The drying room was often used as a shortcut to the other huts. Through the next door on the same side were the wash-hand basins and toilets and from there onwards, on both sides, were the sleeping huts. I was in the first one on the left past the toilets.

In each of these huts were twelve ordinary camp beds made up of a wooden frame with a mesh type base and folding legs about twelve inches high. The beds were already made up with two white linen sheets. The bottom sheet was changed each week. There were two pillows with white pillowcases and two army type blankets. The only protection from the concrete floor was a coconut mat about 4 feet by 2 feet at the side of each bed. Also at the side of each bed was a small wooden locker about 5 feet high, 2 feet 6 inches wide and 18 inches deep. It had shelves on one side and a rail on the other. This locker was where we were expected to keep all our clothes. I kept most of my clean clothes in my suitcase on top of the locker and dirty clothes on the bottom of the locker. This was the only way I could keep my clean and dirty clothes separate.

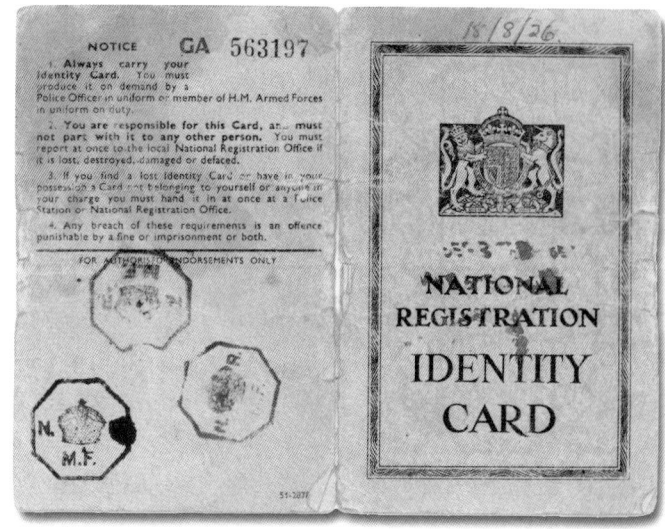

Just below the curve of the ceiling ran a 4-inch hot pipe. This was the only heating in the hut and everyone found it very cold especially during the winter months. I unpacked my suitcase. I was the only one there as my room-mates were still at work. I wondered what they would be like and if I would get on with them. I then remembered how everyone got on at the other hostel and I stopped worrying. They turned out to be great guys and we all got on well together. I freshened myself up and went to the canteen for lunch. I was starving by this time as I hadn't had anything to eat since breakfast at the hostel at Townhill. I had a very nice three-course meal consisting of soup, meat, potatoes and vegetables. This was followed by a sweet.

The Manager, Mr. Lawrence Helliwell, was a former Captain in the Army. He and his office staff organised events within the hostel. They arranged concerts by local organisations and they also arranged bus trips to the theatre in Edinburgh and mystery tours. I found the Manager strict but fair. He would not allow alcohol in the hostel or noise in the sleeping quarters. Other than these two rules we were free to do as we wished.

Talk by a member of the French Resistance

I remember one of the evening events arranged by the office was a talk by a member of the French Resistance or Underground Movement as it was known. This was during his visit to Britain. He spoke of his experiences in France during the Occupation by the Germans. He gave a very interesting talk and spoke excellent English. What I remember most was his introduction. He told us his name was Heintz and his next words were, "do you know the 57 varieties? I am the 58th". He said we wouldn't forget him and I certainly haven't. Some of us went forward to meet him after his talk for a cup of tea and a chat.

The next time I saw him was on the 25th May 2004 on a TV programme called Ten Days to D. Day to mark the 60th Anniversary of the D. Day Landings. He introduced himself as Andre' Heintz spelt with a 't' which was the German spelling. He talked about how excited he was to receive the Coded Message on his homemade radio to say that the invasion had begun. He had shown this to us during his talk. He then had to pass the message on to other members of the Underground Movement/Resistance. They would then help the Allied Forces by cutting telephone lines and blowing up railway lines etc. He went on to say that although he and his sister lived in Caen and had many friends there, he couldn't warn them that the city would be bombed.

He mentioned that his sister was a nurse in the Hospital. He explained how he and his sister soaked two white bed sheets in blood before laying them out to form a cross. This was to let the bombers know that it was a Hospital. Just at that time a plane was passing over and the pilot gave a signal with the plane to let them know that he recognised the sign.

The office staff in the hostel also arranged visits to other hostels such as Comrie and Townhill, which were both in Fife and Armadale in West Lothian. They in turn would visit us at Newtongrange. This would often be on a Monday which was our dance night. We would also challenge each other at darts and table tennis and the home team would supply the refreshments. I was in the darts team and my mate Stan Hever was in the table tennis team. He was a good player. Also on the staff was the Caretaker who was responsible for the girls who cleaned the huts. They made sure everything was spotless and also made our beds every day. They were a fine bunch of girls and were always very clean and smart. The Caretaker was also responsible for waking us for work in the mornings. The kitchen staff supplied us with excellent meals considering that food was rationed. They were always cheerful and most helpful.

Visit to the Lady Victoria

As I was passing the office after lunch one of the girls told me that I had a visitor. It was Mr. Tom Walton the Training Officer for Bevin Boys. I learned later that he was a member of The Mines Rescue Team and had assisted in the rescue of miners when there was an accident in the Lady Victoria in 1945. The Hostel Manager gave us permission to use the reading room where Mr. Walton introduced himself and gave me a brief History of Newtongrange and its association with The Lady Victoria Pit. He also told me that I would be working there and he would be there to help me at any time.

About an hour later we made our way to the pit which was only about 100 yards down the road where we turned left through the gates and made our way to the pit office. When we arrived there I was introduced to the office staff and given my token number. I remember two of the office girls were identical twins about 17 or 18 years old. Both had ginger hair and were very friendly. They promised me a dance at the hostel in the evening. I learned later that a dance was held every Monday evening to help the new Bevin Boys settle in. When we left the office Mr. Walton accompanied me up the steps to the pithead where a man was standing who said, "Hello Tommy, what can I do for you and who is this with you"? I was introduced to Mr. Bob Allan the Foreman. Mr. Walton told him I was a Bevin Boy and would be starting there next morning for two weeks training before going down the pit. He also asked him if he would get someone to teach me the job and to see that I didn't come to any harm.

While I was standing there I watched as the cage arrived at the pithead with hutches full of coal. Mr. Allan saw that I looked surprised to see them coming out of the cage and onto the rails near where we were standing. He explained that someone was at the other side pushing empties onto the cage to be returned to the pit bottom. There was a lot of activity, hutches coming and going in every direction. It was quite frightening. They could see I was a bit worried and assured me that someone would be looking after me all the time. I thought, here I am a young lad 18 years old, starting on what looked a very dangerous job and after a few days training would be going underground to work. I wasn't looking forward to starting work next morning. An hour or so later I returned to the hostel and to my hut. None of my roommates had arrived back from work so I decided to have a walk to Newtongrange and have a look round.

My first visit to Newtongrange Village

Newtongrange was only about 200 yards from the hostel. I crossed the (A7) road and walked towards the village. I was now on what was called Main Street. The first thing I saw was a fruit and confectioner's shop called Scott's. I believe it was owned by Jennie Scott. Next and around the corner was the Palace Picture House. I thought that that would be handy for a night out. As I walked further down the street there were more shops selling a variety of goods. The shops that I remember were Wilkinson's Electrical Goods and Jean Ovens Hardware. This was where I called in to buy a flask and piece box to use for my drink and sandwiches. Both were made of tin as there was no plastic in those days. I would need them for work the next morning.

There were more shops on the same side of the street. A Newsagent owned by Mr. Syme. His son Jacky sometimes served in the shop. A couple of steps up at the back of the shop there was a post office where two girls were serving. One was called Grace who was Mr. Syme's daughter. The other girls name was

Ann Hunter. She was slim with dark hair. If I remember right next door was a Bank and then a Chemist. I found out later that Mr. Walton's daughter Lily worked at the Chemist.

Next to the Chemist shop was Miss Humphries's Drapers and then another Chemist. At the end of the row of shops was Quinto's. As the name suggests, he was Italian and sold ice cream and sweets etc. Across a narrow road that led into a field were a hairdressers and the Miners' Institute. On the other side of the street was the Church of Scotland and this was at the bottom of Sixth Street.

The Church was to play an important part in my future. From there I walked further down the Main Street and came to two rows of houses. If I remember right it was on the second row where I saw there were steel bars across the windows of the first house. I wondered if it was the Police Station.

I continued walking down the street until I came to the Dean Tavern that I later learned was very popular with the miners. On the number of occasions when I visited the Dean it was always busy. Everyone seemed to be talking about work as well as drinking. There were another two or three shops just past the Dean. Turning to the left just past these shops was another street called Station Road. As the name suggests the Railway Station was behind it. There were more shops here including a Co-op. On the other side of this road were more shops. I had now come to a crossroads where there were white gates and a railway crossing.

I found that I could buy almost anything I needed in the shops at Newtongrange. All the shops were on one side of Main Street with houses on the other. Even on my first day I found people very friendly. All the way there and back someone would say hello and the girls in the shops would speak to me when I went in to buy something. They must have known that I was a Bevin Boy from the hostel and had just arrived in the village. I felt a lot better when I returned to the hostel about an hour later.

Meeting my room mates

My roommates still hadn't returned from work so I lay on top of the bed to rest. We didn't have chairs or anything else to sit on. I must have dropped off to sleep as the next thing I knew was when the door opened and three of them arrived. The others were not far behind. They introduced themselves and asked me if I was resting before the dance. It was a quick 'hello, see you in a few minutes', as each one stripped off their dirty clothes, wrapping a towel around them and headed for the showers.

I remember the names of some of them. There was Jimmy Dunn who was in the bed at the top end of the hut from me. I believe he

My room mates and I - taken at the Miner's hostel Newtongrange. Top row: Danny, Jim Dunn, form Motherwell or Hamilton, Jock, ?, ?. Middle row: ?, Stan Hever, lived near Dennison. G. Ralston. Bottom row: Jimmy Graham, from Glasgow. Andy Bathgate.

was an Industrial Chemist from either Motherwell or Hamilton. Across from me was Jimmy Graham. I think he came from Glasgow. He was quite a character. There were also three or four miners from different parts of Scotland. One was Andrew Bathgate. He and I often went for a drink together. He later went to Australia to help his uncle on the farm. We lost touch after a while. There was also Gordon and Jock. I forget their second names. I think they came from the north of Scotland somewhere. When they returned to the hut and while they were changing, we had a chat to get to know each other. They all seemed nice lads and were very friendly. They turned out to be good mates. The others were from different parts of Scotland, mostly from the Glasgow and Motherwell area. As I mentioned earlier, not all of them were Bevin Boys. I think the miners who lived in the Hostel had come to work locally.

One of the first Bevin Boys to move into the Hostel was Robert (Bob) Hall. I believe he came from Jedburgh. His first job was underground in Lingerwood Colliery directly opposite the hostel. He didn't have far to travel to work but I understand he wasn't happy with the type of work he was doing. Fortunately there was a vacancy in the Carpenter's Workshop in the Lady Victoria which was similar to the type of work he was used to back home. He applied for the job and was successful. I learned later that he met and married a local girl and remained in Newtongrange.

After a hard shift, they were ready for something to eat. I joined them in the canteen and had a cup of tea. When we had finished, three or four of us went into the lounge to continue our chat. There were about half a dozen lads sitting on armchairs chatting. Some were sitting at tables playing board games while others were reading. While we were in the lounge, one of the other Bevin Boys started playing the piano. He was an excellent player and could play anything. I envied him his talent. He would often play for us. Sometimes we would sing along. At other times enjoy listening to him playing. I hope that working in the pits didn't damage his hands. He had a great gift.

I learned later that the hostel had been officially opened a few days before I arrived by: Mr. Thomas Johnston MP, Secretary of State for Scotland. Mr. G.H. Henderson, the Secretary to the Department of Health for Scotland and Major S.H. Mackintosh, C.B.E. Regional Controller Scotland (including Northumberland and Durham) of National Service Hostels Corporation Ltd, accompanied him.

The Hostel Dance

At about six o'clock we returned to our hut to get ready for the dance. We went down to the lounge about 7.15p.m. to arrive just before the visitors. The two girls from the office arrived about fifteen minutes later. My roommates were surprised when they both came over to talk to me. I was standing just inside the door and when I sat down they sat on either side of me. They asked me about myself and where I came from. They hadn't met anyone from England before and had never heard of Corby. They asked me why I didn't have an English accent and I explained. After a few dances it was the interval and they joined me in the tearoom for a hot drink. We then returned to the lounge for a few more dances. They were both excellent dancers and very good company. I was reluctant to leave before the dance finished but I gave both girls my apologies saying I wanted an early night as I didn't want to be late for work on my first day. They understood and I knew they would have plenty of dancing partners for the rest of the evening. I enjoyed my first day at Newtongrange.

Working on the Pithead

I was concerned about sleeping late as I didn't have a watch or alarm clock. My mates told me to pin a note on my locker saying what time I wanted to be wakened. I didn't sleep much. I was restless with all sorts of things going through my mind. I could see the hutches travelling at speed on the pithead. I was in a sound sleep when the door burst open and the caretaker shouted, "Wakey, Wakey, First Call"! This was about 5.30a.m. He came round again about 20 minutes later shouting "come on lads, last call"! By this time I was wide awake but I enjoyed those few extra minutes. All the other lads had to get up earlier than me as they had to catch the bus to work. After they left I got ready and then went to the canteen for breakfast.

The menu was a choice of porridge or cereal, egg, sausage, fried bread and as much toast as I could eat. The breakfast was much the same every morning. When I had finished breakfast I went to the kitchen and handed over my tickets and collected my sandwiches for lunch. I was given four thick slices of what we in Corby called 'Scotch Bread'. It was the same shape as the piece box. There was a choice of cheese, spam or jam and also a piece of cake or a biscuit. I also had my flask filled with tea. Cold tea with milk isn't a nice drink with sandwiches so I took cold water for afterwards. Sometimes I would take a flask of tea without milk, which was a pleasant drink.

Now it was time for work. I made my way out of the side door and walked down to the pit through the gates and reported to the office where I collected my tokens. I said hello to the two girls thanking them for their company and for a pleasant evening hoping to see them at the dance the following Monday. For the second time I made my way up the steps to the pithead. I reported to Bob Allan the foreman. I remember he had a bad leg. I expect it was a result of an accident at work. He called one of the lads over and told him to look after me for the rest of the shift. We were at the back of the cage where the full hutches were being pushed off the cage by the empties on the other side. I asked the lad where I could leave my sandwiches and jacket. He pointed to a place in the corner for my sandwiches but suggested I keep my jacket on as it was cold at the pithead.

Our job as we worked together was to guide the hutches round the bend to a chain drive. This then took the hutches up to the top deck where they joined the others from the upper deck of the cage. From there they run down an incline to the weighing machines and then to the Tipplers. I felt really cold there, especially when I was handling the cold hutches all day. My hands never had a chance to get warm. I was glad when the end of the shift came and I could return to the hostel for a hot shower and something warm to eat.

When I returned to work next morning I had to report to the upper deck where I was doing similar work. Part of the shift was pushing empty hutches onto the cage. This was quite heavy work as I had to put enough weight behind the empties to push the full hutches off at the other end. We were kept busy all day and I was very tired by the end of the shift. After I had my shower and something to eat I was so tired that I lay on top of my bed. I was asleep when my roommates arrived.

On the third day I was put on another job. When the hutches pass the weighing machines they run down an incline to the Tipplers. I was shown how to slow down and stop the hutches using Scotches before they reached the tipplers. There were two types. One was made from a steel bar about 1 inch diameter bent round at one end to form a handle about 4 inches diameter (see photo).

The total length was about 14 inches. The bar was pushed between the spokes of the wheel to slow down the hutch. The other Scotch was made of hard wood and also about 14 inches long. It had a handle about 2 inches in diameter and 9 inches long with a 4inch square, tapered at the end. The tapered end would be pushed between the rail and the wheel of the hutch gradually slowing it down before it reached the Tipplers. It was a bit scary at first. I was worried about losing my fingers.

The other lads were experts and taught me the best and safest way to use the Scotches. It took me at least half the shift to be fairly competent. There was always someone nearby looking after me. By the end of the third day I was feeling more relaxed knowing there was always someone there to help if needed. I wondered where I would be working the next day

Entrance to the shaft of the Lady Victoria

On the fourth day I was taken to the Tipplers, they were like cradles. My job was to push a full hutch onto the Tippler. The empty would come off at the other side. I would then lock the full hutch in position and pull the lever at the side. This would turn the Tippler over emptying the coal onto the tables below. Later, when I looked down below I could see that it was mostly women who worked there. They were picking out stones or anything else that should not be mixed with the coal. It looked a very dirty and boring job. Everyone was covered in coal dust. I felt that women should not be doing that type of work but this was war time and women were doing all sort of jobs and doing them well as I had already learned in the Tube Works back home. It was heavy and hard work on the pithead and cold.

By the end of the week my clothes were beginning to suffer from wear and tear from the sharp pieces of steel sticking out of the hutches. My trousers and jacket were too thin for that type of work. I had to do a few repair jobs over the weekend. It was the first time I had thought about it and wished that all us Bevin Boys had been given at least one set of heavy clothing or overalls which would stand up to the work we were expected to do. If we had been called up for the services, we would have been supplied with uniforms and other clothing.

I expected to be on the surface for another week's training but Mr. Walton paid me a visit on the Friday to tell me that there was a job waiting for me underground starting on the Monday. He knew from what I had told him about Muircockhall that I wasn't looking forward to going down on the cage after my experience there.

Taken by my son when we attended the Xmas Dinner 14th December 1999. Putting a Scotch in a wheel to slow down or stop the Hutch.

My last days on the pithead

Mr. Walton explained to me the difference between the shaft and cages at Muircockhall and the Lady Victoria. He told me I would find the journey much smoother. He also explained what I would find when I reached the pit bottom. He said that it was large and well lit. I remember him saying jokingly, "the only thing missing were chandeliers". I felt a bit better after our talk but not a lot. I was still concerned as to whether I would be able to cope. I had the weekend to think and worry about it. He reassured me as much as he could and told me that he would arrange for someone to meet me at the office on Monday morning to look after me and take me to where I would be working. After our talk we went to see the foreman to let him know that I would be leaving the pithead and starting my new job underground on the Monday morning. He said I would still be working on the pithead on Saturday. I didn't know then that Mr. Walton had spoken to Mr. Allan about me and asked if he thought I was ready to start working underground. Mr. Allan had said I was coping well and willing to learn.

Before I left Mr. Allan gave me a word of advice which I found very helpful. He saw that I was carrying my flask and piece box in my hands and suggested that I get an old waistcoat and stitch two pockets inside large enough to hold my flask in one pocket and piece box in the other. It was an excellent suggestion. It left both my hands free for walking to and from my place of work. My aunt Rebecca had a sewing machine and stitched the pockets in the waistcoat for me when I visited my Grandparents at the weekend. While I was there I told my Grandparents that I was going down the pit on the Monday. My Grandfather said not to worry that I had done well so far and would soon settle in and knowing miners as he did, he told me they will help and look after me.

My first day down the Lady Victoria

The day arrived for me to venture underground for the first time at the Lady Victoria. I had to report half an hour earlier to allow for travelling to work. I reported to the office as usual. After giving my check number I received two tokens, a round one and a square one. I was told to give the round one to the banksman before going onto the cage and to hand the other into the office at the end of the shift. This was a safety precaution for all miners to make sure that they were not still down the pit when they should have finished work.

My guide was waiting to take me to where I would be working and we introduced ourselves. His name was Willie Shaw. If I had been asked to describe what a miner would look like I would have described Willie Shaw. We both made our way up the steps towards the cage. I had already collected my lamp from the lamp office, fixed my battery onto my belt and checked my lamp was working before fixing it onto my safety helmet which I had always worn from the first day I started. Most of the other miners wore a soft cap.

With my lamp and battery already in place I was now ready to go onto the cage but before that I had to go though a safety check. The Banksman did this. He asked me if I carried matches or a lighter. As this was my first visit underground he explained the dangers and risk of fire. I understand that he had the authority to make a check by searching anyone if he wished. I told him that I didn't smoke. I knew him from working on the surface for those few days and he knew it was my first day going underground and wished me luck.

I followed the other miners onto the cage and was surprised at the number of men who got on before it was full. I learned later that the cage carried at least 50 men as there were two decks, about 25 on each. I heard the clunk as the gates closed. I was on the other side of them now. The signal was given to the Winding Engineman and then we were off down the shaft. I can't remember feeling nervous or having any particular sensations in my stomach. I was too busy looking around me and at the men beside me. Everyone was quiet. They seemed to me to be just waiting to reach the pit bottom and get to work.

I remember looking at the walls of the shaft. It was circular and very wide and bricked all the way to the bottom. I learned later that it was about 1,600 feet deep. Just think, nearly one third of a mile. I felt it was a long way underground. I often thought about all that weight on top of us. I looked at each corner of the cage where there were wire ropes about 2 inches or more in diameter. They were acting as guides, giving a nice smooth journey to the bottom of the shaft. We passed the other cage on its way up. It was dark except for the lights from our lamps. I had no sensation of travelling anywhere in particular.

I remember thinking I am pleased that I am not going skywards. I believe that I would be more nervous if I had been able to see where I was going. After a time I could feel the cage slowing down and seeing lights as we neared the pit bottom. Gradually the cage came to a halt. I was surprised how smooth the journey was. As I carefully made my way off the cage taking care not to trip over the rails, I looked around me and was amazed at the contrast from the training pit at Muircockhall. I don't know what I had expected but certainly not what I saw. I entered what looked like a large bricked tunnel just under the height of a two-storey building and just under the width of two houses. It looked as if the walls had been painted white at one time but over the years had got dirty from the coal dust.

The pit bottom was well lit and so it was much brighter than I had expected. About 20 yards or more from me were two smaller tunnels about 8ft high and 8 ft wide. I saw later that there was a tunnel coming from another direction. The tunnels were the main haulage where the coal was received from the four different coal seams. These were the Newbattle, Dalhousey and Carrington section where I would be working.

The Splint section used the same haulage road as Carrington. The rails from each section led to the cage where the full hutches would be loaded onto and the empties pushed off at the other side. Then they would be returned to the coal face where they would be refilled. Willie Shaw and I made our way to the haulage road which would take us to Carrington section. He removed his jacket and suggested I do the same. We then put them on a nail in a manhole. He told me that we wouldn't need a jacket as it would be warm enough where we were going but we will need them on our return to the pit bottom. It was always cold at the pit bottom. This was more so in the winter months with the cold air being drawn down the shaft. From there the air would be directed along the main roadway to all sections in the pit, especially to the coalface. I kept my waistcoat on as I found it ideal for carrying my piece box and flask as Mr. Allan had suggested allowing me freedom to use both hands should I trip over something which was always possible down the pit.

Going down on the Bogies

From there we walked to a heavy door which he asked me to open. I needed both hands and a good pull before it opened. When we went through there was another door. I had to remember to close the first door before opening the second. The air was warmer there. Willie Shaw said that we were now in the return air course. It was explained to me later that the air in this section was the impure air returning from the coalface and other parts of the pit. From there it was directed along a roadway, up a steep incline to Lingerwood the pit above and then into a ventilation circuit where the impure air was directed to the surface. This roadway would also provide an alternative means of exit from the Lady Victoria in case of emergency.

I learned later that the reason for this arrangement was that pits were required to have two shafts. One shaft was for normal use and another ventilation shaft that could also be used in an emergency. When the Lady Victoria was planned it was decided that it was only necessary to sink one shaft and use the ventilation shaft of Lingerwood, the pit above us, as the second shaft. As the Lothian Coal Co. owned both pits this would save time and the cost of a second new shaft.

Anyway, returning to the ventilation doors, after going through the second door we entered a roadway about 8 feet high and about the same in width where we made our way to the bogies. These were used to carry the miners nearer to their place of work. The bogies were made up of two or three trucks coupled together, each one holding about a dozen men. They had timber across for seats and were completely open, no top or sides. We both joined the other miners and sat down. The seats were very uncomfortable. I was sitting on the right hand side very close to the wall. I looked for something to hold on to but there was nothing. I wondered what would happen if the bogies stopped suddenly. I expect we would have been shot forward and landed on top of each other or onto the rough floor. I worried about this on the few occasions that I travelled on them.

I remember on one occasion when I was sitting in a similar position my piece-box was caught on something sticking out of the wall. The box opened and my sandwiches landed on the floor leaving me with an empty box. This meant a day without food. Two of my work-mates came to my rescue and shared their sandwiches with me. I thought this was very generous. It would have been more serious had I lost my flask. Water is more precious than food when working down the pit. As soon as the bogies were full, we were off. A wire rope about one inch in diameter was attached to the bogies and the other end was wound around a drum on the haulage engine. When the brakes were released, the weight of the bogies carried us down the incline. This was the first time I felt nervous down the pit. I didn't feel safe. I was expecting the bogies to jump the rails at any time or to run away. I was pleased when they came to a halt. I jumped off as soon as they stopped. All the other miners were going to another section called the Splint.

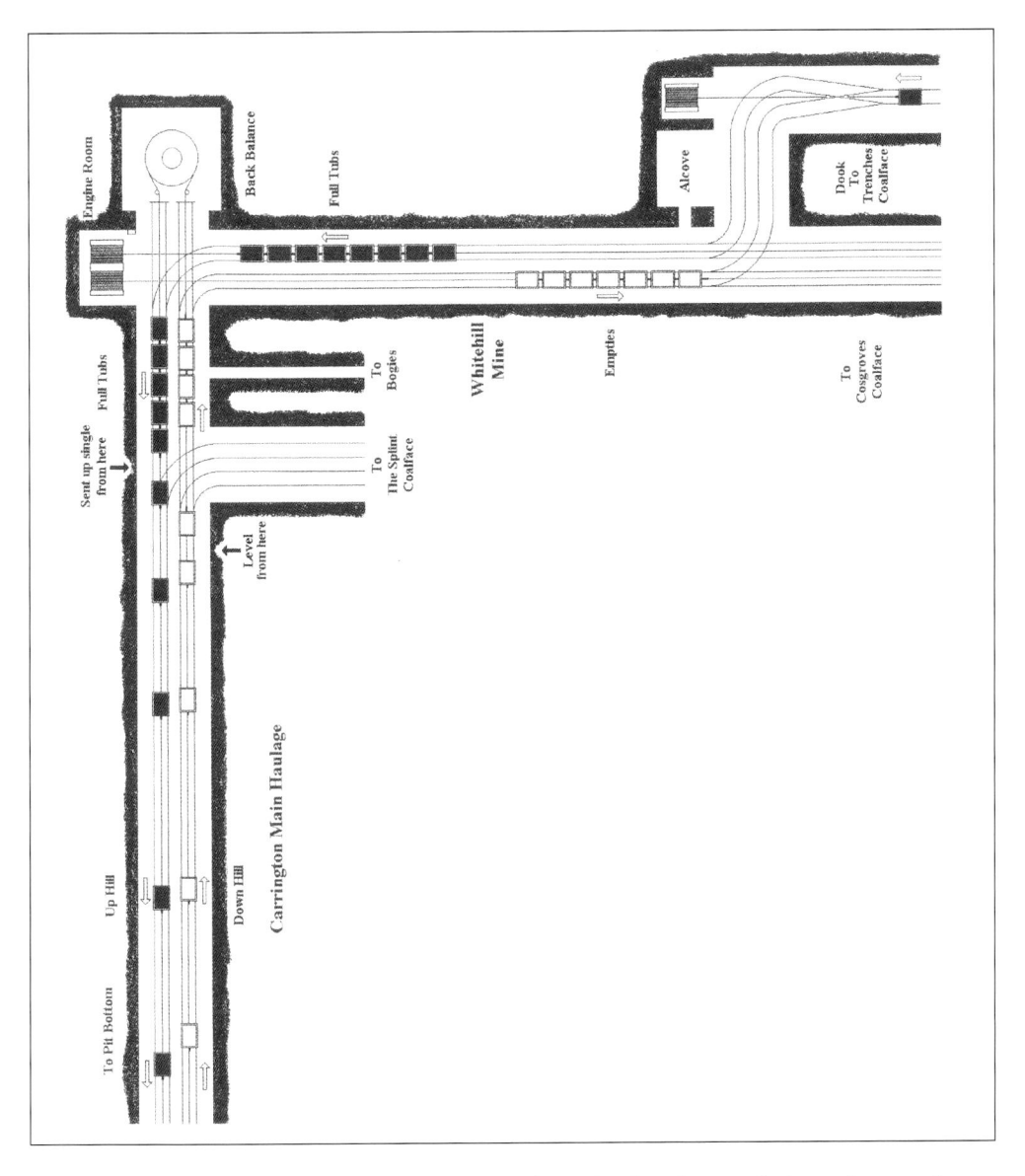

I followed Willie Shaw to an entrance on the left. It was so low that I didn't see it at first. It was only about 2 feet 6 inches high at the most and very narrow, only room for one of us. When I entered the entrance I found it very steep. As

Willie was in front I followed him. We had to crawl most of the way and some places we just slid down. This time I was really nervous. I wondered where we were going and what had I got myself into. I had never experienced anything like it before. I could hardly breathe. I was sweating. I don't know if it was lack of air or if it was just nerves. I felt everything was coming in on me. I tried to be brave and not look worried.

After what seemed like ages we reached the end and walked into a large brick tunnel about 8 feet high and about 10 feet wide. I was so relieved. We stopped for a rest and for me to calm down. When I looked down I saw that running along the floor of the tunnel were two sets of rails with a wire rope moving between each of them. I could see electric lights in the distance in both directions. He told me we were now in the main haulage road. We turned to our right and walked to the end. Willie, who had brought me this far, told me this was where I would be working. A few yards from where we were standing was what was called the Back Balance where the rope went around a pulley. This rope would take the full hutches on their return journey to the pit bottom. Immediately beyond that was a brick wall behind which was what was known as The Great Seam. I was told that this seam had been worked until they came across a fault and had to stop production.

Arriving at Whitehill Mine

I was introduced to Bob Scott in the Engine Room as he was the driver of the haulage engine for Whitehill Mine. He was one of the few miners who carried a pocket watch which came in handy at times as I would lose all sense of time while working there. The engine room was in an alcove on the left of the main haulage. There was also an old type telephone there where we could contact other parts of the pit and the surface. Directly opposite was what was known as Whitehill Mine where I would be working. I next met Tony whose job I would be taking over. This would allow him to return to work at the coalface. I understood Tony's family came from either Poland or Lithuania after the First World War and settled in Newtongrange.

About half an hour later I saw a light in the distance coming along the main haulage road in our direction. It was the Foreman Dave Young going on his rounds. He introduced himself and suggested we sit down for a chat and get to know each other. He was a very tall man well over 6 feet and well built. We always said that he had hands like shovels. He told me Tony would show me the job and that I must not take any risks. He also assured me that I would not be left on my own until I was certain that I was ready to take over and that everyone was there to help me. While we were talking, Tony had taken some empty hutches into the mine in case they were needed and fetched out eight already filled with coal.

By this time Willie Shaw had brought in a dozen empties from the main haulage for us to take inside the mine. Tony as my instructor showed me how to use the haulage clip. It was over 2 feet long with a hook at one end. This was put into the eye of the first hutch. The other end of the clip had two jaws, one with a screw and a shaped handle. The jaws were placed onto the haulage rope which was about an inch in diameter. When the handles were tightened the jaws gripped the rope and the hutches started moving. Each hutch was attached to the one in front.

Showing the type of job I was doing.

The mine was at least half a mile long with arched steel girders and bricked all the way. Some parts of the roof were better than others. About 20 yards in from the main haulage the height was about 5 feet. I could see water dripping from the roof. Other parts were about 6 feet high. The sides were narrower in some places especially at the entrance where the hutches would rub against the wall.

All along the sides of the mine were manholes. These were about 5 feet high and 2 foot 6 inches wide and 2 ft deep. Little did I know at the time I would be glad of one of them. Along the full length of one side of the mine, about 4 ft up from the floor, were two low voltage wires about 6 inches apart. These went all the way to the engine room. When rubbed together a bell sounded in the engine room. Once was the signal to stop and two for starting.

Now back to work. When the empties were clipped onto the rope we walked alongside them into the inside of the mine making sure to duck when the roof became lower. At the inside of the mine we came to an incline. Tony told me to stand back while he showed me what to do. When just over half of the hutches were over the incline he unscrewed the clip from the rope and then took the hook out of the eye of the first hutch and hung the clip over it. The hutches would then run down the incline by their own weight to the end of the haulage and round a corner. When they were needed they would be clipped onto another rope by Charlie Dickson who would send them down a dook, a very steep incline to the coal face where they would be filled with coal at a conveyor and then pulled back up and returned to me.

About four yards past the bend on the rails was the back balance where the rope from the empty side of the rails went round before going back outwards towards the main haulage. On the right side of the back balance was a sump where water was collected before being pumped up to the next stage. About four yards behind the back balance were two large wooden doors. At this time I didn't know what was behind them and I wasn't curious enough to find out. When there were about 8 full hutches ready for me I would clip them onto the haulage rope and take them out to the other end of the mine where I would take the clip off again at an incline. The hutches would then run by their own weight round the bend onto the main haulage where they would be clipped onto the main haulage rope by Willie Shaw and taken out to another junction. Willie Currie and his two assistants, Bobby Dyer and Pete Dickson, would clip the full hutches onto the haulage rope one at a time where they would travel to the pit bottom.

I later met Jimmy Sharpe the maintenance fitter or Jimmy Sherpe as everyone called him. I can still see him now as he walked in between the two sets of rails carrying his tool bag on his shoulder. He introduced himself to me and I told him my name was George. He wasn't very tall and was slim built. What I remember about him most is that he was always cheerful with a smile on his face. He always called me Dodd every morning when we met. He would say "hi Dodd, how are you this morning?"

I later met Piper McQueen who was responsible for repairing the haulage rope when it was damaged. I also met Jockie Slater and the electrician. If I remember right his name was Sandy Smith. I found everyone so friendly and helpful and as a stranger it meant so much to me being away from home and working in a strange environment. It was most likely the first time they had worked with someone who wasn't local. I soon settled into my new job especially knowing I was among friends.

When Tony and I went in with our next set of hutches, the Fireman Johnny Patterson, was sitting in an alcove making out his report. He had already been to the coalface checking for safety and whatever else he had to do. As I had to wait for more full hutches to make up our load before taking them out to the

PHOTO OF MYSELF AND THREE WORKMATES WHEN I WAS A BEVIN BOY IN THE LADY VICTORIA NEWTONGRANGE.

PIPER McQUEEN - WILLIE SHAW - PETE DICKSON

main haulage, he suggested I join him for a chat and get to know each other before he returned to the coalface. He became a good friend to me and helped me a lot while we worked together. Everything seemed to be going well on my first day until, near the end of the shift, when two of the full hutches came off the rails. I was shown various methods of getting them back onto the rails. They were very heavy. Each one held about a ton of coal. Often we had to lift the hutch onto the rails with our backs against it, one end at a time. When I was on my own I had to get someone to help me as it too heavy for one person.

By the end of the first day I was almost ready to be left on my own. I found the days very long and lonely. It wasn't as bad on the first day as I had Tony for company but on most days after that the only time I saw anyone was when I returned to the engine room at the main haulage where I would see Willie Shaw or Bob Scott. The others were always just passing through on their way to the coalface. I was always pleased to see a light coming towards me. I knew then I would have company for a few minutes at least. I remember a few days after I started, it was in the morning and I was in the engine room talking to the foreman Davy Young, when suddenly there was a terrific rumble above us. I looked up and around us ready to run. I was really scared. I thought the roof was coming down. He just sat there calm as you like, "It's alright" he said, "just the earth moving above us". He had heard it many times before. I heard it often afterwards but it still made me nervous. I was always ready to run just in case the roof was coming down.

Near the end of the shift on my first day I saw a lot of lights coming out Whitehill Mine towards me. They were the men from the coalface on their way to the pit bottom and going home. Those of us working on the haulage would stay on a bit longer to get as many full hutches to the pit bottom as possible and enough empties to the coal face ready for the face workers starting next morning. When it was our time to leave I wasn't looking forward to crawling back up the narrow road we had come down in the morning or travelling back up on the bogies. I was relieved when I was told that we would be walking to the pit bottom up the main haulage.

One of the lads gave me one of his home made walking sticks and showed me how to walk on the haulage rope while it was moving. He taught me how to use the stick to keep my balance by pushing it against the wall. I found it much easier than walking on the roadway which was very uneven with metal sleepers, pulleys and rails. I became quite an expert after a time. It was a long walk to the pit bottom. I don't know how far, perhaps a couple of miles uphill. This was how I travelled to and from work afterwards except for the few occasions when I travelled on the bogies.

Sometimes on our walks we would come across hutches that had come off the rails. When they were full of coal we needed extra help. We were usually aware of it beforehand as the rope would be jumping and we would have to get off. One of us would press the two wires together to signal the engine driver to stop the haulage rope. Everyone would help to lift the hutches back on the rails. The signal was then given to restart the haulage. We would then continue our journey to the pit bottom. I soon learned that this was how miners worked, everyone helping each other.

When we reached the pit bottom I put on my jacket. I could feel the cold air coming down the shaft. I took my time as I walked towards the cage having a good look around to get familiar with the area. I still couldn't believe just how big and bright it was in the pit bottom. I then joined the others ready to go onto the cage, hesitating a bit before stepping on. When the gates closed we were on our way up the shaft. I wondered if I would feel different this time. This was my first journey to the surface. It was a different sensation. The cage seemed to be travelling faster this time, or perhaps I just imagined it. Soon it was slowing down as we neared the surface. When we reached the top I heard the clunk as the safety gates lifted to let us off. I followed the others, carefully stepping off the cage.

My first shift was over. It didn't seem so long since I was on my way down. Everyone made their way down the steps. I followed them on their way to the Lamp Station where we handed in our lamps for the battery to be re-charged ready for next morning. I handed my token into the office. This would let them know that I had finished my shift.

After that it didn't worry me travelling on the cage except during the winter months when for the first time I saw large icicles hanging down the walls of the shaft a short way down from the pit head. Each one was at least 6 ft long and 6 to 8 inches in diameter at the top going down to a point. I had visions of them breaking off and falling down the shaft and coming through the cage. Because of this, during the winter months I always tried to travel on the bottom deck just in case. I think what caused the icicles to form was there was a pipe all the way round the top of the shaft which had small holes giving off steam.

At the end of my first day I had handed in my token and made my way back to the hostel and to my hut where I stripped off, wrapped a towel around my waist and went to the showers. This became the daily routine. I felt the cold go through me as I put my feet on the concrete floor. We didn't have slippers in those days as we couldn't afford the coupons. I ran to the showers, black all over with coal dust. My legs were the worst caused by disturbing the coal dust as I walked on the haulage road. Next morning I was told to tie a piece of string round the bottom of my trouser legs. This helped quite a bit. After I had showered and dressed I went for my dinner. I was ready for something to eat but more thirsty than hungry. One flask of water or tea isn't much to last for a whole day.

After finishing my meal I went for a walk to Newtongrange to get stamps. I went into the paper shop and up the steps to the post office where two girls were serving. By this time they recognised me. After getting the stamps I returned to the hostel to write a letter home and let my family know how I got on with my first shift underground. It was almost dark by this time. One of the many disadvantages of working in the coal mines during the winter months was it is dark in the mornings going to work and dark soon after finishing. The only time we saw much daylight was at weekends.

The Hostel Dance

When I returned to the hostel I went to the quiet room to write my letter home as I wanted to get it posted as soon as possible. I walked back down to the post office and dropped it in the post box. When I returned to my hut the other lads were dressed. They were curious to know how I got on with my first shift underground and what type of work I was doing but most of all about the conditions I was working under. Afterwards I had time for a rest before getting dressed for the dance in the evening so I lay on top of the bed. I must have been tired after my day's work as I dropped off to sleep and was wakened when my mates returned from the canteen.

I went to the dance in the evening and this was always very popular. I think the girls enjoyed themselves because there was never any trouble. Girls came from Newtongrange and also from Arniston, Gorebridge, Gowkshill and Birkinside. Although I didn't like working in the pits I enjoyed the social life. I made many friends and everyone was so kind and friendly. My friend Stan Hever and I went out regularly together going to other dance halls in and around Newtongrange. We had some enjoyable evenings dancing in the Masonic Hall in Dalkeith. It was very popular with other Bevin Boys. Many of the girls we met there didn't attend the dances in the hostel so we made many new friends. I think what helped us most was that we were newcomers to the area. Some of the girls who attended the hostel dance would invite us to their local dance hall. I went to Vogrie dancing a few times and enjoyed it very much.

Looking back I think that the dance hall I enjoyed most was Craigesk. It was situated at the outskirts of Newtongrange under the Arches of the main Edinburgh to London railway line. It was a big hall with a good floor for dancing. The band was also very good. If I remember rightly it was called Jock Thomson's band. I'm sorry if I have got the name wrong but it was a long time ago. The band played a good selection of dances in addition to the usual quickstep, foxtrot, waltz, and an occasional tango. They also played a selection of old time dances. Also, eight-some reels, old time waltzes amongst others, depending on the mood of the dancers on the night. One dance that would get everyone joining in was called The Hokey Cokey. I have never seen it danced since. Very seldom did we have any trouble at the dances. I suppose this can be put down to the fact that alcohol was not sold on the premises only soft drinks and pies. One of the advantages of going to the dancing at Craigesk was that it wasn't too far to walk back to the hostel, especially during the blackout.

When we went to the dancing at Dalkeith we had to walk home to Newtongrange through what was known locally as the Peth. It was a back road past Newbattle Abbey and a Cemetery. Along part of the road there was a wood on either side. It was Eerie at night but a lovely walk during the day. I walked it often during my years at Newtongrange. It was a convenient shortcut.

My second day at work

On my second day at work I decided to go early. I collected my tokens and lamp as usual and went down the cage with the other miners. As I got off the cage I met up with Bobby Dyer who also worked in Carrington Section. After removing our jackets I followed him into the haulage road. The rope hadn't started by this time as it was too early so we carried on walking. After about 10 minutes or so the rope started moving so we stepped on it. I found this was much easier walking uphill than downhill. A few times my foot slipped off the rope on the way down until I got used to it. As I was early that morning and had a few minutes to spare, Bobby introduced me to Bill Currie who was the Contractor in charge at that section of the main haulage. He was a tall man and well built and we became good friends during my time in the pits. I later met his family.

He and his men, Bobby Dyer and Pete Dickson, (everyone called him 'Pate') clipped the full hutches onto the haulage rope one at a time. They then sent them on their way to the pit bottom. They also supplied the Splint Section with empty hutches and when they were returned filled with coal they sent them to the pit bottom. As they had to supply both sections they were kept busy.

It was still early when I arrived at my section so I had time to have a chat with Bob Scott. He mentioned that he always liked to be early as he had a bad back and had to take his time getting to work. He told me he injured his back while working at the coal face and took the job as engine driver because he was unable to return to work there. There were empties ready to go inside but I thought it better to wait for Tony. He arrived a few minutes later and asked me if I thought I was ready to work on my own. When I told him I thought I was, he said that we had better wait until we had a word with the foreman. While we were waiting he let me clip on the empties. When we arrived inside he let me bring out the full hutches, keeping a careful eye on me all the time. When we returned to the main haulage the foreman was sitting in the engine room. After a few words with Tony, the foreman asked me if I thought I was ready to work on my own and I said yes. He asked if I was sure and I again said yes. He then told Tony that he could return to his job at the coalface. He was quite pleased as it meant more money for him but I didn't envy him one bit.

As there were no empties ready to go inside, Tony left us and went on his own. He had to report to Alex Trench who was the contractor for that section. It was called Trenchs after him. When the empties arrived I phoned into the inside of the mine to say that I would be leaving with them. The Fireman answered the phone saying he was just leaving to return to the coalface. He told me that he would ask Charlie Dickson to wait for me coming in to make sure I would be all right. I am pleased to say that everything went well. I became more confident as the day went on. One thing I did find out after Tony left was that it was darker in the mine with only my lamp. After a few hours I began to feel hungry and thought it was time for lunch. On my journey out with the empties I went into the engine room and asked Bob Scott if it was lunch time, he said yes and joined me.

Just as we sat down we had a visitor. It was a man I hadn't seen before. I would say that he was past retirement age, short and looked as if he had spent all his working days in the pits. He was carrying an oil can and a scraper about 18 inches long. He told me his job was cleaning out the pulleys and oiling them to make sure that they run freely. This was to prevent grooves wearing on them and damaging the wire rope. I saw him most days after that. He must have had to walk miles each day. He was responsible for all the pulleys from the pit bottom to the coalface in Carrington Section. Perhaps that is what kept him fit. I wish I could remember his name. He was a nice old gentleman and we got on very well together and always had a chat.

I soon realised that it was a lonely job being on my own most of the shift. I was always pleased when I saw a light coming towards me. I knew that I would have a little company. I was kept very busy and it was soon time for a break. We didn't have any set time for eating. I tried to fit it in to suit the job. Bob Scott and I usually ate together in the engine room to keep each other company. Occasionally, when it was convenient, or if I was waiting for full hutches to come up from Trench's, I would have my break at the other end of the mine. I didn't like eating on my own. Sometimes, while eating my sandwiches there, I would see pairs of eyes looking at me from the far corner. It was the rats wanting to share my lunch. I am pleased to say that they kept their distance and would just stare.

Someone was employed by the company to put poison in the sections to keep down the rat population. The poison made them thirsty and they would make for the nearest water. We would often find them lying dead beside the water sump opposite. I remember one unpleasant occasion when a rat fell behind the brickwork of the alcove and was trapped. This was where the fireman would sometimes join me while making out his report or I would sometimes join him when I was waiting for full hutches to come up from the coalface. After that incident we had to keep out of the alcove for more than a week until the smell dispersed.

Everything went better than I had expected. I took my time and the others, Willie Shaw at the main haulage and Charlie Dickson at the inside of the mine, kept an eye on me, helping when it was needed. As a result I soon settled in. The shift passed quicker than I had expected and I was surprised when I saw the lights coming from inside the mine. It was the men from the coalface coming out at the end of their shift. Soon it would be time for me to go home. I was very pleased with the way I had coped on my second day.

At the end of my shift I returned to my hut in the hostel and as on my first day I stripped off my work clothes and wrapped a towel around myself and made my way to the showers. This time I was in for a shock. While I was under the shower I turned round to see two of the Cleaning Ladies walking past. They just looked straight ahead, saying 'we called out'. I didn't know what they meant. I was so embarrassed. I quickly dried myself and returned to my hut. When my roommates came in from work I told them what had happened. They just laughed and explained that the ladies used the shower area as a short cut through to the other huts instead of going outside especially during the winter months. I asked why someone didn't tell me and they just said that they wanted me to be caught out. The young girl who cleaned our hut apologised when I saw her later that day.

This happened on quite a few occasions while I was staying in the hostel. I learned that the arrangement was that the ladies would call out, "we're coming through", as they came through the door but we didn't always hear them. After a time we got used to them coming through and would just turn our backs.

Near the end of the week, on different days, I had two slight mishaps. The first one was when I came out of the mine with some full hutches. We called it a 'Rake' of hutches but I don't know why. It was just after lunch and because of the break there were twelve waiting for me inside the mine instead of the usual eight. When I reached the outside of the mine and because of the extra load, I had to bring the hutches further over the incline before taking off the rope clip. As a result I was struggling to unscrew the clip and get it off the rope before it went under the junction of the main haulage. It was fortunate that Willie Shaw was there still keeping an eye on me. He was quicker than I was and pulled me out of the way and managed to take the clip off just in time. I breathed a sigh of relief and thanked him.
Something similar happened a few days later just as I was unscrewing the clip. Part of the rope which had been repaired by the rope splicer earlier got stuck fast in the jaws of the clip. I couldn't unscrew it any further and this time there was no one there to help me. I knew that the clip was heading for underneath the junction and I couldn't do anything to stop it. The only thing left for me to do was to run towards the engine room to tell Bob Scott to stop the haulage rope and hope for the best. Fortunately, from where he was sitting he could see what was happening and stopped the rope just as the clip had reached the junction

preventing further damage to the rope. Unfortunately we couldn't do anything to stop the hutches running down the incline. As a result the clip was damaged and two or three of the hutches came off the rails. As we were on our own and the hutches were full we had to phone for help to lift them back onto the rails. With the extra help it didn't take long and I am pleased to say that none of the hutches were damaged.

It was a very lonely job as I mentioned earlier and although there were lights at the junction of the main haulage it was dark about twenty yards inside the mine. I often wondered what it would be like if my lamp went out. I was to find out sooner than I expected. It happened on two occasions and I was left in complete darkness. Fortunately it was only for a short time but I was scared. Darkness down a coalmine is different from above ground. There is no moon or stars to help. It is pitch black and you lose all sense of direction. I remember I found it very frightening the first time it happened to me. I was taking empties inside the mine and just where the roof gets lower I bumped my head on one of the girders knocking off my helmet with my lamp still attached. They fell to the floor.

I was in complete darkness holding the back of my neck where I had jarred it. I was frightened to move as the hutches were still moving. I could feel them rubbing against me. I couldn't call for help as no one would hear me. After a few minutes that seemed much longer, I was aware that all the hutches had passed. I put my hand round to where the battery was attached to the back of my belt and then felt for the cable and hoped for the best. As I lifted the cable there was a flicker of light. Much to my relief the light had stayed on. It had landed face down in the coal dust covering the front of the lamp making it dark. I quickly put my helmet back on my head and hurried on to catch up with the empties. On the second occasion when it happened it was more frightening. The light had gone out as I hit my lamp on one of the girders. I was in a panic. I didn't know what to do. I put my hand up to the lamp and flicked the switch. To my relief the light came on, perhaps I hadn't switched it on properly.

The end of my first week underground couldn't come quickly enough as I was broke. I hadn't had any wages since I left Muircockhall. I had to work what was called, a week's lie time. The practice was that when you started a new job you had to work two weeks before being paid the first week's wages. At the end of my shift I went over to the main office which was across the road from the pit gates. Round the left side and at the back was the wages department. I handed my wage slip to the wages clerk expecting to get a wage packet. Instead I was handed a small tin about 2 inches diameter and 2 inches deep. When I took the lid off my wages were inside. Two pound notes were folded over and the coins on top, a total of about £2.10 shillings (£2.50). I took my wages out and handed the tin back. I expect using a tin for the wages was the company's way of saving paper.

I learned later that the wages clerk's name was Helen Stirling. I got to know her after a couple of weeks and invited her to the Hostel dance. She said that she would think about it. One evening she turned up. I went to meet her as she came through the door and asked her to dance. We had a few more dances together. My mate Stan Hever was with me and he also danced with Helen. Near the end of the evening she said it was time for her to go home. She mentioned earlier that she lived on Main Street at the bottom of Newtongrange across from the Dean Tavern. As it was during the blackout, I asked her if she would like me to walk home with her and she said yes. Stan was standing beside me and said he could come with us and we both agreed. I think Stan had a soft spot for her. We had a steady walk through the village. When we reached the Dean we sat on the wall chatting for a while.

Lothian Coal Co., Main Office

When she told me her father was a policeman I mentioned about seeing the bars on the window of a house when I was walking through the village and was curious about what they were. She told me it was the Police Station and the window with the bars was one of the two cells. She told me her father was the Police Sergeant and that they had lived in the police station before moving into the house beside the Park Gates. I learned from her sister Jessie that her father was later promoted to Inspector. She gave me the two photos of her father to include in my book. You will notice that he was a very tall man. The earlier photo was taken when he served in the village and the other, while on a special duty on the Forth Bridge. Jessie later married Mr. Walton's son John.

Visiting Chapelhall

On a particular Saturday I went to work as usual. It was a shorter shift and we finished about 1.00 p.m. I then went to the hostel to get showered, changed and packed ready to visit my grandparents for the weekend. They were always anxious to know how I was getting on at work. They always told me I would be able to cope well and they had a lot of faith in me. I checked out of the hostel about an hour later telling the girl in the office I would be back on the Sunday about 8 00 p.m. I usually left the hostel about 2 o'clock and caught the bus to Edinburgh. From there I would catch the Glasgow bus to Airdrie and then I would take the bus to Chapelhall. The journey would take me about 2 hours.

Doing my laundry

When I arrived at my grandparents I would make myself something to eat before doing my washing. I couldn't expect my Granny to do it for me as she was 84 years old. I feel that I should mention here how clothes were washed in the days before washing machines. The method we used was a rubbing board and hard soap. If I remember right it was green fairy soap. The laundry was done in the kitchen in two oblong sinks alongside each other. One was deeper than the other with a wringer attached between them. When the clothes were washed they were put into the other sink for rinsing and then put through the wringer to get as much water as possible out before hanging them out to dry. Also in the kitchen was a zinc gas boiler which I would use to boil my clothes when necessary. If the weather allowed I would hang my washing outside to dry but if it was wet it was hung on the pulley in the kitchen. Every house had them and they were very useful. I would do my ironing on the Sunday afternoon. We didn't have electric irons then and the irons were made of steel or cast iron and heated on the gas stove. I would always do my darning and other repairs at the hostel. I became quite an expert.

My Grand Parents

56

Needing new clothes

The days and weeks were passing and I was finding it difficult to keep up with the wear and tear of my clothes both financially and with the shortage of clothing coupons. My socks were wearing fast with all the walking I had to do every day. My darning was quite good but not good enough as the holes were appearing regularly. My shirts and trousers (I had two pairs of each) were too thin to stand up to the wear and tear from the ragged edges of the steel hutches. I remember thinking at the time that it was very unfair the Bevin Boys were not given an allowance for the type of clothing we would need for working in the coal mines. The clothes I needed were two thick navy vests and shirts, three pairs of thick socks and two pairs of special trousers called Moleskins. To buy them I needed to save up which wasn't easy on the low wages we Bevin Boys were getting. I was also a bit short of clothing coupons

The weeks were passing quickly and it was nearly Christmas. If I remember right we were given one day's holiday so I decided to spend it with my Grandparents in Chapelhall. They were pleased to see me as always. When I got out of bed on Christmas morning, I found three pairs of thick socks in my stocking which they had hung up. It was just what I needed. There were also enough clothing coupons from my Grandfather to help me with the other clothing I was short of. I didn't have the money to get everything at the same time but after a few weeks I had everything I needed. As an ex-miner my Grandfather knew how important it was to have the proper clothing. They were a wonderful couple and gave me a lot of advice and support at the time.

Going Dancing

While I was there at the weekend I would go to the dancing on the Saturday evenings at the Welfare Hall in Chapelhall. I would often meet up with old friends I had known before moving to Corby. I remember one Saturday evening in particular when I was there. I was sitting talking to two girls I had worked beside before moving to Corby when two of my old school friends came over to talk to us. One was in Army uniform and the other was in the Navy. They asked me in a loud voice so that everyone in the hall could hear why I was not in uniform. I remember my thoughts when Mr. Heinz told us that he was a member of the Underground. I thought at the time that I was also in an underground movement. I stood up and whispered to them both saying that my job is 'hush hush' and that I was a member of an underground movement and not allowed to wear uniform. They just looked at me not knowing what to say turned and walked away. I sat down again.

At other times I would go to the pictures at one of the cinemas which were very popular during the war years. One of them was the Odeon in Airdrie where I worked from the age of 15 for about a year. After going to the Welfare dancing a few times I decided to attend some of the other dance halls that I had gone to before moving to Corby.

A visit to Airdrie Palais

On this particular Saturday I decided to pay a visit to the Airdrie Palais as I had gone there often in the past. It was a lovely hall with a very good dance floor and an excellent band. I had not been there for a couple of years and so it was not surprising that I found there were many unfamiliar faces amongst the dancers. I decided to sit out a couple of the dances before deciding whom I should ask for a dance. Some girls have regular dancing partners and I didn't want to upset anyone. When I crossed the floor to ask a girl to dance I was disappointed as someone was there before me and I had to walk back.

While I was watching the first dance I noticed a girl who looked familiar but I couldn't remember where I had seen her before. She was a lovely dancer and I watched her all the way through the dance. She had lovely dark hair and like most of the other girls there she was wearing a long evening dress. It was a lovely shade of red and she was quite tall for a girl. I made up my mind to ask her for a dance. When the next dance was announced I made my way across the floor to ask her to dance. Again I was too late, someone else arrived before me. The same thing happened on the next occasion so once again I had to return to the other side of the dance floor. I tried again on two more occasions but I was disappointed. Each time I would look at her to show my disappointment and choose someone else to dance with. By this time I had noticed that she danced with a different partner each time so I came to the conclusion that she didn't have a regular partner and was on her own.

It was getting near the interval when the M.C. announced that the next dance would be a 'Ladies Excuse Me'. I looked across the floor but the girl in the red dress had gone. I asked another girl to dance and after the first round of the dance someone tapped my dancing partner on the shoulder and said "excuse me". I was delighted to see that it was the Lady in Red who was cutting in. I told her how pleased I was she had cut in as I had tried to get a dance with her a few times. She said that she had noticed and seen how disappointed I looked each time. After dancing for a few minutes she mentioned that she had a feeling she knew me from somewhere. She told me that she was pleased that I didn't give up.

When I asked where she had gone to she told me that when the M.C. had announced the next dance would be a Ladies Excuse me she left the dance and went into the lounge until the dance started hoping that she would get a chance to dance with me. I asked her name and she told me it was Margaret. I told her that was one of my favourite names. I was just going to introduce myself when she said, 'you're George aren't you'. I said 'yes', do we know each other'? We never stopped talking all the way through the dance. At the end of the dance we went into the lounge for a cold drink and to continue our conversation. When we were in the lounge she told me that we knew each other when I worked in the Odeon Cinema in Airdrie. We had spoken to each other often when she went to the pictures there. I apologised for not remembering straight away but after a few minutes talking I did. I said that she had changed so much in those few years as girls do. I did tell her that although I didn't recognise her at the time I knew there was something familiar about her when I first saw her on the dance floor.

After two more dances we went up to the balcony to continue our conversation. She asked me where I had gone to as she had missed me and wondered what had happened. I told her about moving to Corby and that from there I had been sent back to Scotland to work in the pits as a Bevin Boy. It was the first time that she had heard of them. I said just think, if I had not been called up as a Bevin Boy you wouldn't have known what happened to me and we would never have met again. At the end of the dance I walked her home as was the custom. Margaret lived on an estate called Gartlee. It was on my way to Chapelhall so I wouldn't be too late getting home. I had walked through that estate often when I worked in the Odeon so I knew my way.

We arranged to meet the following Saturday and for old times sake we decided to go to the Odeon Cinema. It brought back happy memories for me as I hadn't been back since moving away. We had a very nice time at the pictures and like the previous Saturday I walked her home. We didn't make any arrangements to meet afterwards. Perhaps we thought that we would bump into each other again and I wasn't always certain when I would be able to get back to Chapelhall at the weekend.

A visit to Dennison Palais

On a few occasions I would meet up with my mate Stan Hever another Bevin Boy who lived in the hostel when he went home for the weekend. He lived in Alexander Parade Glasgow and we would go to the dancing at Dennison Palais.

As I didn't know the area I thought it would be better to wait until the summer months when it was daylight longer before paying my first visit. I knew the centre of Glasgow well including the area around George Square, Sauchiehall Street, Central Station and the bus station. As I hadn't been to

Danny, George Ralston & Stan Hever. Bevin Boys. At Newtongrange.

Dennison before, Stan arranged to meet me at the bus station. We had a cup of tea nearby before going to the Palais. Afterwards I was able to make my own way there. It was a lovely dance hall with a terrific band and some lovely dancers. I always enjoyed myself there. Unfortunately I always had to leave early to catch the Tramcar back to Airdrie. I always looked forward to travelling on the Tramcar even although the journey was a bit rough as it rumbled on the rails, swaying from side to side. It was also very noisy. I always found it exciting and an enjoyable way to travel and they run later than the buses.

I remember that after I got on the tram on that first night it started to get dark. All the streetlights were on and the houses were all lit up. Many of the householders hadn't closed their curtains or drawn their blinds and it was like that all the way to Airdrie. What a contrast to the Blackout. It was a lovely sight and one of the many signs that the war was over. I was the only one left on the tram when it reached its destination at Airdrie Terminus where it would begin its return journey. Tramcars didn't turn around. The driver would move to the other end of the tram and move the backs of the seats backwards in the opposite direction. By this time I had missed the last bus to Chapelhall but I didn't mind as it only took me about twenty minutes to walk there.

Bellshill Dancing

When my Auntie Rebecca and Uncle Tam moved from Chapelhall to New Stevenson I would occasionally stay with them at the weekend. When I was there I would sometimes go to the pictures in Motherwell or the dancing in Holytown or Bellshill. I remember one Saturday night at the dancing in Bellshill I saw a girl I recognised from somewhere. When I asked her to dance and mentioned this she told me that she had seen me at the dancing in the Raven Hall in Corby. She told me she was on holiday and living with relatives in Mossend. We had a few dances together and talked a lot about Corby. I thought at the time how nice it was to meet someone from back home. At the end of the evening I walked her home as I knew the area well as I had relatives who lived nearby. As she had just arrived that morning and had another week's holiday I arranged to meet her following Saturday. I saw her couple of times afterwards when I was on holiday in Corby.

Meeting Robert in Airdrie

There is one visit to my Grandparents that I will always remember as it was so unusual and so unexpected. It happened on one of the Saturday's that I had decided to go to the pictures. I had just got off the bus at Airdrie Cross and went to see which film was showing at the cinema. Fortunately as it turned out the film didn't appeal to me and I made my way back to the Cross. On my way there I was surprised to see my twin brother Robert walking towards me. Neither of us could believe our eyes. He told me that he had a few days leave and decided that as our Grandparents were

Jim Sneddon, Robert and George

getting on in years he would pay them a visit and spend a few days with them. He didn't know when he would be back again. It was a pure coincidence. Neither of us knew we would be there that weekend. We decided to go straight to see our Grandparents as I knew that it would be a lovely surprise for them.

They were so delighted when we walked in the door. It was so unexpected, especially when they didn't know when they would see Robert again. We decided to take the opportunity while he was on leave to visit Holytown Cemetery. We went to visit the grave of our Mother who died when we were only nine years old and our little sister Margaret, who died when she was only 2 years and six months old. I decided to have an extra day off work and returned on the Monday. Robert had to return to camp the next day. It was his last visit before being sent to the Far East on V.J. Day 1945. It was more than three years before I saw him again. During that weekend I remember our granny saying to him that she had a feeling she wouldn't see him again. Sadly she was right as she passed away about 2 years later while he was in Malaya.

A visit to Armadale Hostel

Ian Campbell one of the Bevin Boys I met at Muircockhall would sometimes join me at my Grandparents in Chapelhall at the weekends. They liked Ian and were always pleased to see him. I mentioned earlier that Bevin Boys and their friends from other hostels would visit us and we would visit them. On one of the visits we met two girls who worked in the Hostel in Armadale and they invited me to visit them there. On one of Ian's visits to Chapelhall we decided to call in to see them on our way to back to Edinburgh.

They were pleased to see us and we had tea and cakes in a tearoom. Ian left before me as he had to catch an earlier bus in Edinburgh for Dunfermline. I decided to catch a later bus which was a mistake as I missed the last bus from Edinburgh to Newtongrange. I was stranded for the night and wondered what I should do when I remembered there was a Y.M.C.A. on Princes Street. When I called there I explained that I was a Bevin Boy and missed the bus to Newtongrange where I lived in the Miners' Hostel. I let them see my National Service Card and was given a bed for the night for the sum of one shilling but no food. In the morning I went to St. Andrews Square to catch the bus to Newtongrange. By the time I arrived at the Hostel it was too late for me to go to work. I had breakfast and then went to bed for a couple of hours as I didn't sleep well at the YMCA. Needless to say that was my last visit to the Hostel in Armadale.

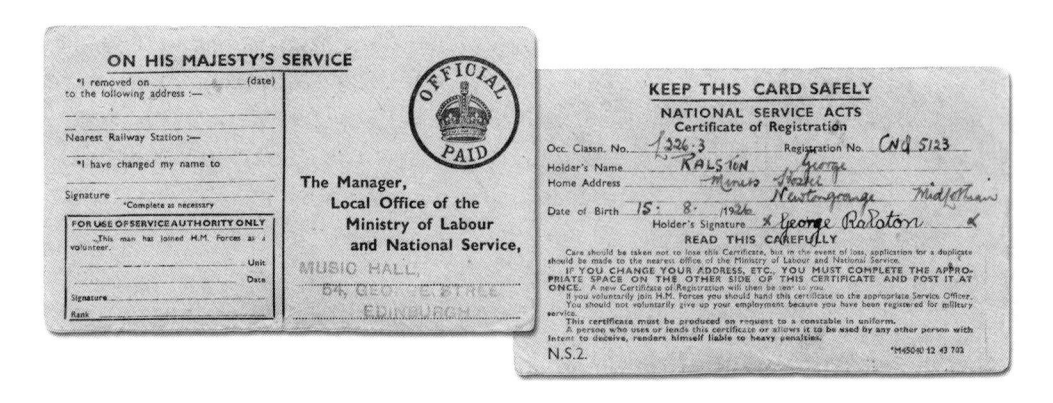

My Accident

Every day down the pit was much the same until the middle of April 1945. I had been to the hostel dance as usual on the Monday evening. The last dance was always a 'Ladies Choice'. I was asked for this dance by one of the girls I had danced with on a few occasions that evening. It was the first time she had been to the hostel dance and many of the lads were keen to dance with her especially as she was an excellent dancer. I was delighted when she asked me for the last waltz. At the end of the dance I offered to see her home. We didn't have cars in those days and the buses stopped running early so it meant walking. As that evening was the first time we had met I didn't know she lived in Birkinside, which is about four miles from Newtongrange. It was a long walk there and back and seemed to take ages. As a result it was late when I arrived back at the hostel.

As I was late going to bed I was tired when the caretaker came to waken us in the morning. I didn't feel like going to work I was still half asleep. After talking myself into it I decided to get up and make the effort, although it would have been better if I had stayed in bed. I had a quick wash and a hurried breakfast and then a rush to the pit office to collect my tokens and lamp. Taking the steps to the pithead two at a time I just managed to catch the last cage down.

When I reached the pit bottom I made my way to the bogies hoping that they would get me to work quicker. I was in luck. The bogies were at the top of the dook ready. I made it just in time to take a seat before they left. When the bogies stopped I jumped off and hurried to the small entrance of the mine that led to the main haulage. I was in such a hurry I forgot how low the roof was and bumped my head as I slid down the slope. When I reached the main haulage I hurried towards the engine room. Everything that morning was a mad rush and I was out of breath when I arrived at my job. Bob Scott the engine driver thought I was having the day off as I always reported early for work. Charlie Dickson had phoned out earlier to say that there were twelve full hutches waiting for me inside the mine. I wasn't very happy about this. I was always concerned that the men at the coalface would be waiting for empties.

As there were empty hutches ready to go inside I didn't want to waste any more time so in a rush I clipped them onto the rope and made my way inside. When I reached the incline at the inside of the mine I was still in a hurry. When I unscrewed the clip from the rope it slipped out of my hand before I was able to get the hook out of the eye of the hutch. As I pulled the clip towards me it fell behind my legs pulling me to my knees and dragging me along the ground between the two sets of rails. By this time the hutches were moving on their own and gathering speed all the time. I couldn't do anything to stop them. I could feel the pain in my knees and legs with being dragged along the rough road and the ends of the steel sleepers.

I could see the road between the rails getting narrower and the full hutches on the other set of rails getting nearer. I had visions of being crushed between the hutches. I was really getting worried. I didn't know what to do except to keep holding on to the front hutch as I was being dragged along. Just before I reached the full hutches I saw a deep gap between the rails and sleepers. At that moment, with a last effort, I managed to pull myself clear and throw myself into a manhole on the opposite side of the roadway. Just as I was clear the clip that was being dragged along caught the wheels of the full hutches on the opposite rails and stopped.. The empties jumped the rails landing on top of each other just where I would have been.

Everything happened so quickly. It was later when I realised that if I hadn't been able to pull myself clear I would have been underneath the hutches. I was also lucky that my helmet and lamp stayed on my head all the time and I was able to see everything that was happening. My lucky charm was with me that day.

My mate Charlie Dickson, who was waiting for the empties, saw what was happening from a distance but there was nothing he could do. The hutches were in his way. He stopped the haulage rope and came to find me. Before he could help me he had to climb over the hutches. I heard him call my name and then call out, "where are you"? When he couldn't see me he thought I was underneath the hutches. Charlie was surprised when I answered him. It was then he realised I was in the manhole. He told me to stay where I was and he would go for help. By this time my knees were getting more painful as they were bleeding and black with coal dust from being dragged along the rough road. I was shaking and out of breath but relieved.

After what seemed like ages, Johnny Paterson the Fireman arrived from the coalface. He too had to climb over the hutches to reach me in the manhole. As he was also the First Aider he struggled into the manhole beside me to dress my wounds. There wasn't much room for the two of us. There are no facilities down the pit for cleaning wounds so he applied sterile dressings to my knees and legs and made sure the wounds were well covered. The legs of my moleskin trousers were black with the coal dust and in tatters. I knew that I would need a new pair and I would have to give up valuable clothing coupons for them but that was the least of my problems.

Davy Young the foreman had been at the haulage engine with Bob Scott when he was told that there had been an accident. He arrived soon after and asked me what happened. When he saw the hutches lying on top of each other he wondered how I had managed to get clear. He was delighted that I had managed

Photograph from Page 26

Photograph from Page 26

Photograph from Page 27

Photograph from Page 38

Photograph from Page 39

Photograph from Page 45

Photograph from Page 55

Photograph from Page 31

1 December 1943 the Government with Ernest Bevin as Minister of Labour and National Service announced a blind ballot directing 10% of all men registering for Military Service to be directed to work underground in the deep coal mines of the United Kingdom.

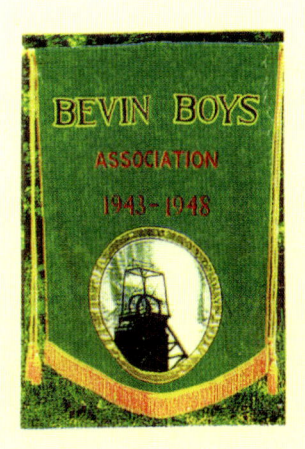

The Association was formed to create a record of those who contributed to the World War II effort by working underground in the coal mines, and to gain recognition for the war service of its members during the period 1943 to 1948. A total of 21,800 were effected

BEVIN BOYS ASSOCIATION
record the
Life Membership of
George Ralston
who completed his National Service after 4 years working in the mining area of
Lady Victoria Scotland
after completing training at

Muircockhall
Scotland

Elizabeth Finsberg
PRESIDENT B.B.A

Philip Wood
CHAIRMAN B.B.A

Picture from Page 9

Photograph from Page 108

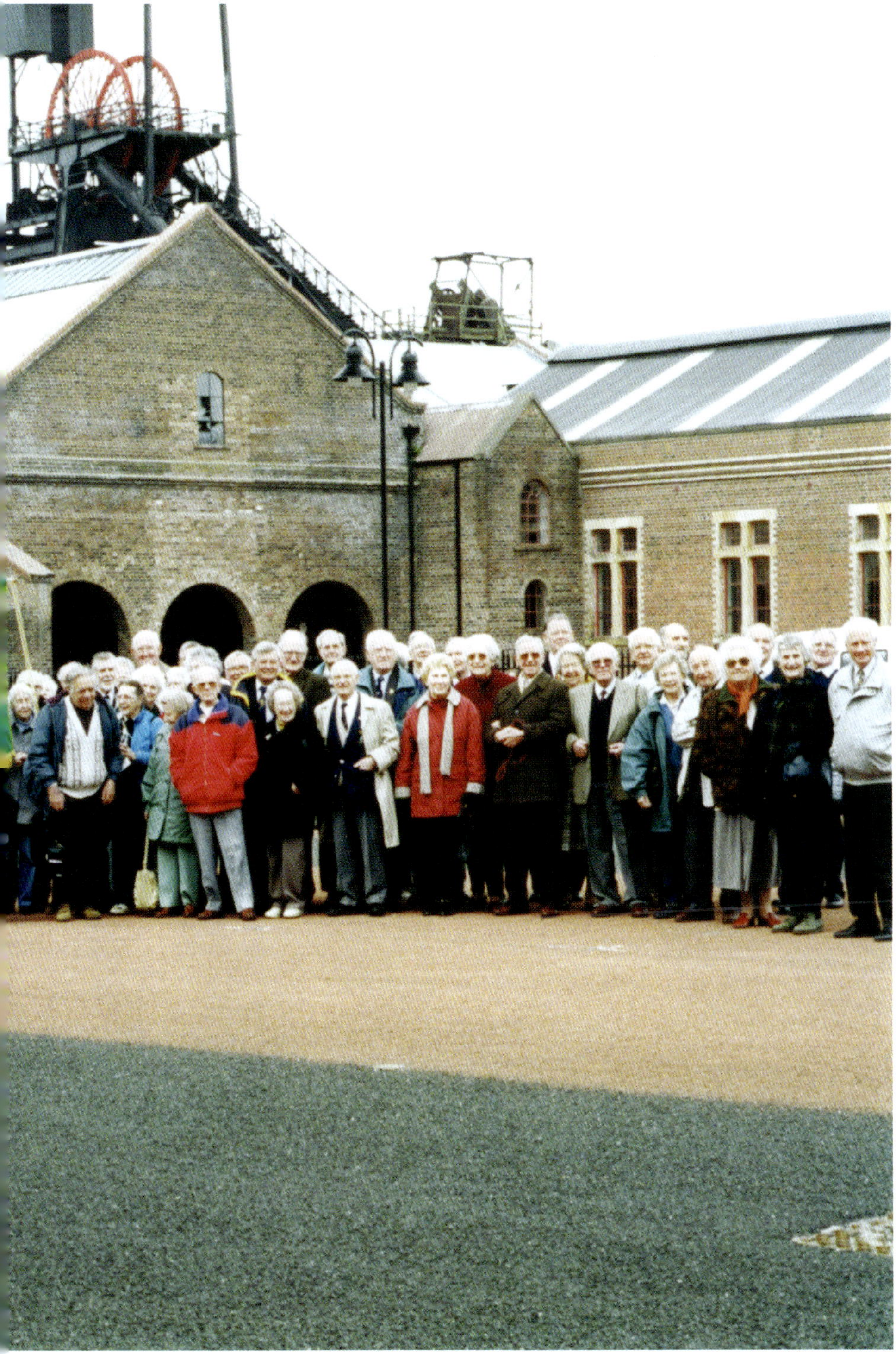

Photograph from Page 109

My Accident

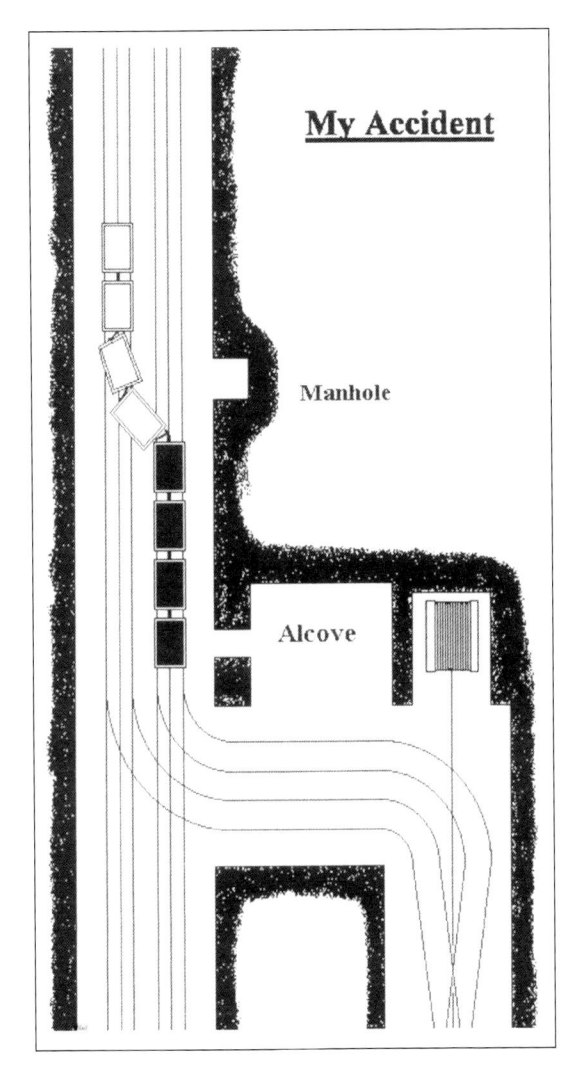

(diagram labels: Manhole, Alcove)

to escape from more serious injuries. Thinking about my accident later I realised that it was fortunate that Charlie Dickson was there waiting for me to bring in the empties otherwise I could have been lying in the manhole for quite a time waiting for someone to find me especially as I was unable to move and climb over the hutches to get help. I wasn't able to walk so the foreman arranged for a flat bogie to be sent in from the main haulage to take me to the pit bottom.

One of the miner's, Walter Anderson, accompanied me. He chatted all the way up the haulage road to take my mind off the accident. He sensed that it was starting to trouble me. My knees were getting more painful and I was beginning to feel cold. I could have done with my jacket then but I had left it in a manhole at the pit bottom.

Walter and I became good friends afterwards. It must have been about two hours after my accident when we reached the pit bottom where it was colder still. I was glad to put on a jacket but I still felt cold. A few minutes after reaching the pit bottom the cage arrived. The empties were taken off and the bogie I had been travelling on was pushed onto the cage. Walter accompanied me to the pithead. The banksman gave the signal to the winding engine man that men were travelling so that he would know to reduce the speed of the cage travelling to the surface. From there I was taken to the hostel sick bay.

The nurse and her young assistant cleaned my wounds and made sure that I had a bath. I needed two baths to get rid of all the coal dust. My legs were too painful to stand under the shower. The nurse sent for Doctor Roulston who was the local doctor and he gave me a sick note for time off work. I had to stay in bed for a couple of days to have my wounds dressed and to rest my injured legs. On the third day I managed to hobble around. I knew that I would not be able to work for a few weeks. As I couldn't afford to stay in the hostel with no wages coming in I decided to go home to Corby until I was ready to return to work.

On the fourth day I was fit enough to travel on the bus to Dalkeith and go to the Labour Exchange to see about a travel warrant for the train to Corby. The clerk behind the counter could see that I wasn't fit for working down the pit but I had to show him my sick note from the doctor to prove it. If I remember right we were allowed three travel warrants a year. I then returned to the hostel to check out telling the girl in the office that I was going home to Corby until I was fit to return. I also had to report to the wages department and show them my sick note. I decided to travel during the night hoping that the trains wouldn't be so busy. I left Newtongrange early to give me plenty of time to catch the evening train at Waverley Station.

Soon after I arrived at the station to pick up my rail ticket the train pulled in. Most of the other passengers were of the same mind and there was a mad rush to get a seat. I wasn't able to keep up with the others but I still managed to get a seat. It helped that the train was leaving from Waverley Station and had arrived empty. There were two empty seats in the carriage and I was able to rest my leg on the seat beside me but not for long. When the train arrived at the next stop it soon filled up. I could see that the corridor was full and lots of coming and going. Some passengers were getting on the train and others struggling to get off at each station. It was like that the whole journey. Fortunately everyone in my carriage was travelling all the way to London so we were not disturbed much. I was able to rest my leg nearly all the way to Corby.

V.E. Day Celebrations

This was my first visit home since I was called up eight months earlier. I was quite excited and looking forward to seeing my family and some of my old friends. Everyone was pleased to see me and asked me about my work in the coal mines and about my accident. After the long journey I was very tired and all I wanted to do was go to bed. My Dad was at work so I was able to have a few hours sleep before he came home.

When the war in Europe ended on the 5th May, I had been home nearly three weeks. I was fortunate to be able to take part in the V.E. Day celebrations at home. This was a great occasion not only for those of us in Britain but also for everyone all over Europe and in the U.S.S.R. I wondered how my mates in the hostel and my friends in Newtongrange were celebrating this great day. In Corby there were parties in every street. We would go from one party to the other and was always made welcome. Everyone was singing and dancing. I don't know where all the food came from but there was plenty to eat and drink, mostly soft drinks. The parties were mainly for the children and they all thoroughly enjoyed themselves. They hadn't known anything like it before. The parties went on all day.

In the evening most of the teenagers and adults went to Stewarts & Lloyds Welfare grounds where there was a large bonfire. Everyone was singing and dancing and we were so excited and happy. Many of us went to the Welfare Dance Hall afterwards to finish off the evening. The celebrations went on all through the night somewhere or other. At long last the war with Germany was over. I was so happy to be home to celebrate even if it was as a result of my accident.

The announcement of the end of the war was not such a surprise as for days before hand we were being told on the radio of the advance of the Allied Forces in Germany and of the capture of many war prisoners. We were also hearing of the capture of the many towns and cities on the way to Berlin. If we were in the cinema at the time a news flash would appear on the screens and everyone would let out a huge cheer. The same would happen if we were in the dance hall. The M.C. would tell us about any advances that had been made by the Allied Forces. Again there would be huge cheers. It was a very exciting time for everyone not only in Corby but I am certain all over the country. We were all waiting for the announcement of the end of the war at any time. When it did come it was a wonderful feeling and relief. There was such joy everywhere. What a wonderful experience it was.

A few days after the celebrations ended I felt that I was ready to return to work at the Lady Victoria. I was feeling much better. There were other reasons too but the main one was I was short of money and restricted in going places. The other reason was that all my mates in Corby were still away in the forces and not expected home on leave. My other mates were at Newtongrange and I was fed up going around on my own especially when my injured legs had healed up. I went to the Labour Exchange in Corby on the Friday to collect my travel warrant telling them that I was ready for work and would be returning to Newtongrange.

Returning to Newtongrange

I left Corby Station to travel back on the Saturday evening. I had to change at Kettering and I had a struggle to get on the train. It was packed as usual and I found it difficult to get any rest on the long journey to Edinburgh. I was tired when I arrived at Waverley Station early on the Sunday morning but after a quick cup of tea and a sandwich I felt refreshed. I walked up the steps from the station to Princes Street and it was very windy. Sometimes the wind could be so strong there that if you were caught unawares, it could blow you off your feet. I had a good look around me as I took a steady walk across Princes Street to St. Andrews Square where I caught the bus to Newtongrange. After about twenty minutes journey I arrived at the hostel and reported at the office to let them know I was back and ready to start work on the Monday morning. It didn't seem any time since I had left. I was delighted when the office girl told me that my accommodation was still waiting for me. This was in the same hut and bed and everything in my locker was as I had left it. All my room mates were still there. They were surprised to see me as I had been away so long. They thought I had decided not to come back and I said no such luck.

When I returned to work on the Monday morning everyone was pleased to see me back fit and well. Walter Anderson who was my relief during my absence was able to return to his job at the coal face. Before he left I thanked him for his kindness and company on my journey up the main haulage after my accident. I also thanked John Paterson the Fireman who gave me first aid and of course, Charlie Dickson who found me and came to my assistance when the accident first happened. I also thanked the foreman for his help when he arrived.

He asked Walter to take over for an hour so that we could have a chat about the accident. I explained everything that happened as I wasn't likely to forget it. He told me that when he saw the hutches lying on top of each other he couldn't understand how I managed to pull myself clear. I told him it was a last effort and that someone must have been looking after me. I apologised for the mess that I had left for him but he said that it didn't matter as everything was soon cleared and there was no damage done.

I was a bit nervous to start with especially when I arrived inside the mine with the first eight empties. Walter was there to keep an eye on me when I took the clip off the first hutch where the accident happened. After the empties had run down the incline I had a look around the area for the first time since my accident. The memories came back to me but they were blurred. I felt grateful that I had escaped more serious injuries. It seemed only a short time ago. I was a bit cautious for a couple of hours until I settled down. I decided, no more late nights during the week!

I remember meeting a man on my first day back who I hadn't seen before. I thought that he was about fifty years old. He introduced himself but unfortunately I can't remember his name. It was when I came out to the main haulage with a load of full hutches just before my lunch break. The first thing I noticed was that everything looked so much brighter, it was so white. I asked him what he had done to make everything look so bright. The walls and floor were covered with a white powder.

As it was lunch time and I had some time to spare he suggested we sit down for a few minutes and he would explain. He told me that the finely powdered dust he was scattering all over the roadways was called Stone Dusting. He went on to explain that when the stone dust is mixed with coal dust it reduces the risk of an explosion. The finely powdered coal dust can be just as dangerous as gas, both can cause explosions. Before leaving he collected some samples of dust to take back to the Labs. I took it for granted that that was where he worked. He told me that samples of dust are taken regularly to be examined by Chemists. As a result, explosions caused by coal dust were rare in those days.

It was while we were talking that he asked me if I had heard about the serious accident that had occurred in the Lady Victoria on the 26th April while I was away. I asked him what had happened and he told me that there had been an explosion in the Splint Section and that there were four fatalities. I wasn't told the miners names and exactly what had happened until I made enquiries later. I also learned that my Training Officer, Mr. Tom Walton who I knew was a member of the Mines Rescue Team had assisted in the rescue of the miners after the accident. Sadly it was too late to save the men.

After about twenty minutes or so, Willie Shaw arrived with the empties and it was time for me to start back to work. It was a funny sort of day, sometimes I felt that I hadn't been away and at other times I felt unsettled. It seemed to take me longer to do some things. I was glad when there was a quiet spell so that I could rest my legs. I was beginning to feel a bit tired. I suppose I wasn't used to so much walking. I was kept quite busy after the break and was surprised and relieved when I saw the lights coming out the mine in my direction. It was the men from the coal face. I knew then I would soon be joining them on the way home. My legs were starting to ache a bit and I wasn't looking forward to the long walk up the main haulage to the pit bottom.

When I arrived back at the hostel I had a quick shower and changed ready for something to eat. I decided to lie on my bed for a few minutes before going to the dining room. I must have fallen into a deep sleep as the next thing I new was when some of my room mates arrived in from work and disturbed me. I decided to stay where I was and join them for dinner.

I went to the hostel dance in the evening as usual but I left early as I wanted an early night. I must have slept sound as the next thing I heard was. "Wakey Wakey, First Call"! It was the caretaker on his rounds. I closed my eyes with relief knowing I had a few more minutes before he would be back. My second day back to work was better. I soon got back into the swing of things.

Summer Holidays

I was only back at work a few weeks when I was due for my week summer holiday. If I remember right it was the first week in July.1945. The holiday was called Trades Week. As I was going to be off work for a week I decided to go back home to Corby even if it was only a few weeks since I was there. It was good to be back again especially as my injuries had healed and I was able to go dancing. I also had the company of some of my mates who were home on leave.

The week soon passed and I was on my way back to Newtongrange, and to work. Even although the war in Europe was over the trains were still packed with service men and women going on leave or returning to camp. It was a terrible journey, still taking about 11 or 12 hours. I arrived back at the hostel on the Sunday ready to start work on the Monday morning. Like the other Bevin Boys, it always took me a day or two to settle down. They too were unsettled after being home for only a short time.

V.J. Day

The days and weeks passed quickly and soon it was the middle of August and I was looking forward to celebrating my 19th birthday on the 15th. I didn't know at the time just how special the day would be. I went to bed early on the evening of the 14th. I was awakened from a sound sleep by one of my roommates. He shook me saying, "George, the Prime Minister (Mr. Attlee) will be making a special broadcast at Midnight". The dining room was packed ready and waiting to hear what he had to say. We weren't expecting to hear what he had to tell us, but it was a wonderful surprise. The broadcast was to tell us that the war with Japan was over and the day was to be a National Holiday. I thought what a lovely birthday present, one I shall always remember. Everyone was cheering. We were so happy and excited. We decided there and then to celebrate. There was nothing to stop us as we had our own band in the hostel so we didn't have a problem.

All the doors and windows in the lounge were opened wide. The band got together and played as loud as possible. Soon the girls and some boys arrived from the village to join us in our celebrations, which went on for hours. Everyone was dancing and singing. The celebrations were still going on when I went to my hut for a few hours sleep. When I arrived all the beds were piled on top of each other just like a pyramid, fortunately none were damaged. I sorted one out for myself and left the others.

When I woke up after a couple of hours sleep some of my roommates were packing their cases ready to go home. They thought as I did that now the war was over we would be released from the coalmines and allowed to go home. As soon as they were packed some of them started to make their way home but as it was a National Holiday there were no buses running. Those who came from the Glasgow and Hamilton area hitchhiked to Edinburgh hoping that they would be able to catch a train to Glasgow. Those who did manage to get home had to return as their working days in the pits weren't over. Little did we know then that we had three more years to serve in the pits as Bevin Boys.

I learned later that while I was celebrating the end of the war in the Far East my brother Robert was on a ship to be sent there. First he was sent to India and from there to Malaya. I didn't see him until three years later when we were both De-mobbed. At that time I wasn't too bothered about going home even if I had been allowed to. I had met a girl at the celebrations that morning. I liked her and wanted to get to know her better. Her name was Lily Walton. I asked if her father was Tom Walton, our training officer and .she said yes. She was with her friend Ella Maxton. I had met Lily once before at the hostel dance. At the time she was with her sister Joan who was home on leave from the W.A.A.F.s and her cousin Irene Henshaw. It was before my accident and I hadn't seen her since.

We arranged to meet later at about 1 o'clock at the bottom of Sixth Street where she lived. It was across from the Church. When we met we decided to have a walk through the park which was only a few minutes from there. We spent a couple of

George and Lily - Taken after VJ Day 1945

hours or more walking along the footpaths talking and admiring the lovely flowerbeds and sitting on the grass. The lawns, flowerbeds and everything in the park were well looked after. They were a credit to the caretaker who looked after them. After a time we sat for a rest and chat in the Band Stand just getting to know each other. While watching the children playing on the swings I remember there was a lovely Rockery in the park where we sat for a while on the large stones. The time passed quickly and soon it was time for Lily to go home for her dinner and for me to return to the hostel for mine. We visited the park often together while I lived at Newtongrange.

We arranged to meet again later at Gowkshill road-end just outside the hostel. When we met there we decided to go for a walk. As I didn't know the area I asked Lily to decide where we should walk. We went from there to what is called Arniston Toll where there was a garage. We turned right there and just kept walking. I had no idea where we were as I hadn't been in that area before. We never stopped talking. Somewhere around there we crossed a bridge where there was a big house standing back behind a large wall. I think that it was called Dalhousie Castle and had quite a history. We carried on walking and found ourselves coming out under the railway viaduct at the bottom of Newtongrange. I knew where I was then as I had been to the dancing at Craigesk a few yards up the road.

We were enjoying each other's company and as it was still daylight we both thought it was too early to go home. We crossed the road and walked through a gateway into what I learned later is called the Red Woods. We continued walking along the footpath. Everything was quiet and peaceful. I stopped at the edge of the path taking care not to slip down the steep drop. Beneath where we were standing the drop was covered with trees, shrubs and long thick grass leading down to a brook. I think it ran into the river Esk. About 10 feet down from where we were standing there was a narrow footpath where at regular intervals there were wooden seats for visitors to sit and rest. As we walked through the woods I thought to myself that it wouldn't be safe walking through here when it was dark.

Soon we found ourselves at the end of the woods and coming out at what was called the Peth, a short cut between Newtongrange and Dalkeith. We walked from there to the White Gates, through the park again and then to Lily's house at the bottom of Sixth Street. By this time it was starting to get dark. It had been a long day and like me Lily had to go to work in the morning. While we were walking she told me that she worked in the Chemists just past the paper shop in the village. I would often visit her there after finishing work. We later had our photo taken on the steps at the back of the shop. We must have walked many miles that day, seeing places I hadn't seen before. Along with the end of the war, this helped to make my birthday a special day.

First Aid Training

It was now a few weeks after V.J. DAY and I was talking to Johnny Paterson the fireman. We were talking about first aid and how important I thought it was especially down the coalmines. I told him how it helped me when I had my accident. We had been talking about it for two weeks or more. During that time he told me he attended first aid classes in Dalkeith and that a course would be running there starting September. He asked me if I was interested enough to come along and I said yes. The classes were run by members of the St. Andrews Ambulance Association and held in one of the rooms at the L.N.E.R. Railway Station in Dalkeith.

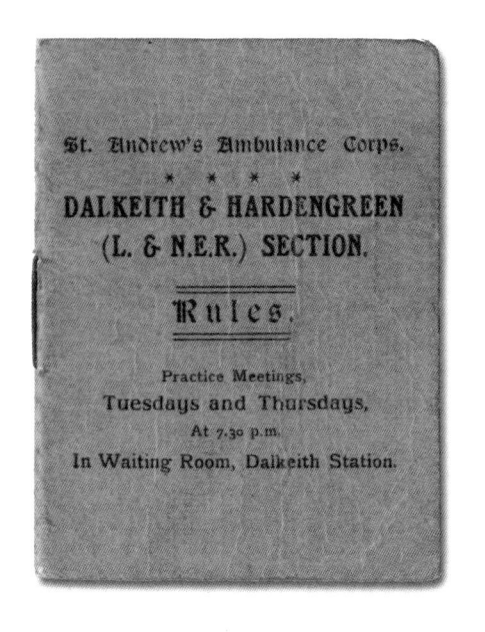

St. Andrew's Ambulance Corps.
* * * *
DALKEITH & HARDENGREEN
(L. & N.E.R.) SECTION.

Rules.

Practice Meetings,
Tuesdays and Thursdays,
At 7.30 p.m.
In Waiting Room, Dalkeith Station.

I joined the course and the weeks passed very quickly. I enjoyed it very much, learning more than I had expected. The course ran for three months and I passed my exams early January 1946. At the end of the exam night Mr. Finlay, the class secretary, told us that a special evening would be arranged for the presentation of certificates. He said that if we wished we could bring a friend. When the evening was arranged I asked my friend Lily if she would be my partner for the night. She said that she wasn't sure, as she didn't think she had anything suitable to wear for the evening. I understood as clothes were still on ration.

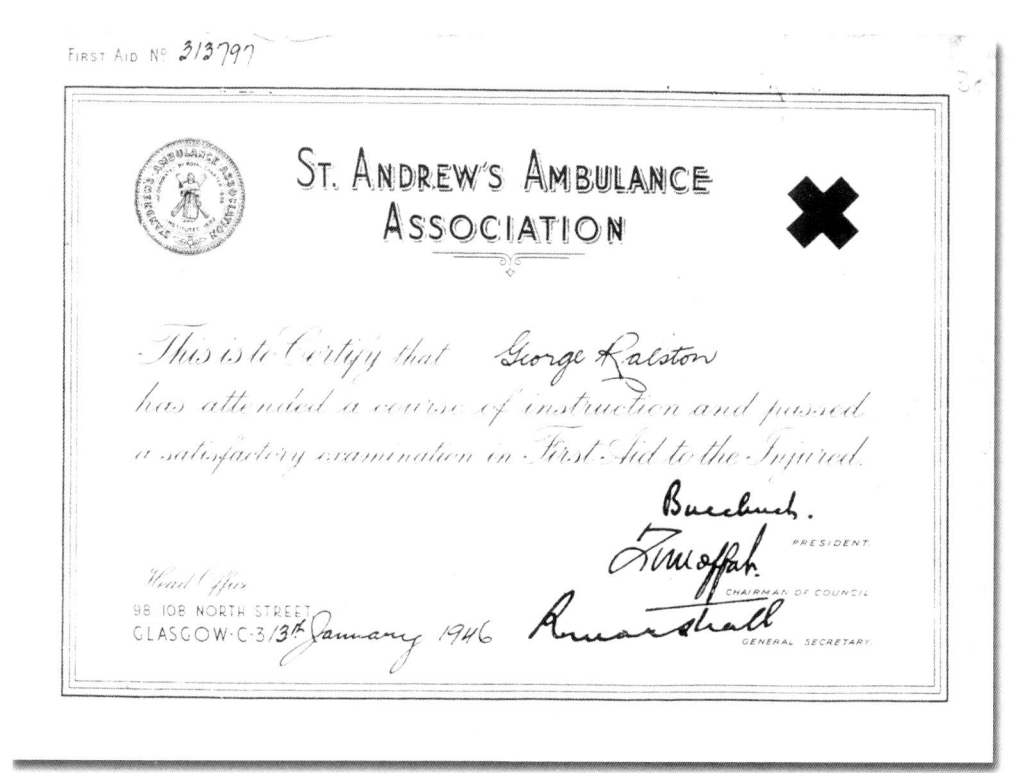

First Aid No. 313797

ST. ANDREW'S AMBULANCE ASSOCIATION

This is to Certify that George Ralston has attended a course of instruction and passed a satisfactory examination in First Aid to the Injured.

Buccleuch.
PRESIDENT.

CHAIRMAN OF COUNCIL

Head Office
98-108 NORTH STREET
GLASGOW-C-3 /3th January 1946

GENERAL SECRETARY.

A few days later she told me that she would like to go with me. She had a look round some shops and she bought some material to make a dress. I wasn't allowed to see the dress until it was finished. I remember it was a long dress, light green colour. Lily looked lovely on the night. I felt good to be in her company. A room was booked in one of the Hotels in Dalkeith for the presentations. After the usual introductions the food was served. We had an excellent meal followed by the presentation of certificates and other awards. I felt really good when my name was called to collect my certificate. It was the first certificate I had ever received. It was a very enjoyable evening ending with dancing.

Little did I know that this was to be the beginning of 50 years first aid service. I joined the St. John Ambulance Brigade when I returned to Corby retiring as Area Commissioner. I shall always be grateful to Johnny Paterson for getting me interested in first aid. Sadly he died during the time I worked in the pits. I had lost a good friend. When I visited Dalkeith a few years later I saw that the railway station where I had learned my first aid had been demolished and a bus station built in its place.

1946 was a bad year for Lily and her family. I remember one evening early in the year when Lily and I were sitting in the park. I noticed that she was very upset about something. After a lot of persuading, she told me that her dad was ill and all the family were worried about him. I don't think she knew how ill he really was at the time. His condition got worse over the next few months.

Lily's mother must have been shocked when his condition deteriorated. Sadly he died on the 26th June. He was buried at the end of the month when everyone in the village was getting ready to go on their annual holidays.
To add to her worry, Lily's sister Joan was away in the W.A.A.F.S and her brother John was serving overseas in the R.A.F. It was fortunate for her mother that Lily and her younger brother Alan were living at home at the time. Joan and John were given special leave to come home to be with the family.

I was upset too, not only for the family but Mr. Walton was very kind and helpful to me during the early part of my training. Many of the other Bevin Boys in the hostel who knew Mr. Walton were also sorry to hear of the loss of a popular Training Officer.

Soon after passing my exams the foreman asked me if I would be interested in becoming the First Aider in Carrington section. He said that it would be a big help as the fireman spent most of his time at or near the coal face and it was always better to have another First Aider in the section should there be an accident while he was away. I accepted his offer. The added responsibility gave me confidence and a feeling of importance. Later when the section was having Safety meetings I was always asked to join them. The foreman felt that as a First Aider I should be involved. The meetings would last about an hour and a half. It also gave me some overtime, which was always welcome. I was also learning something about Safety in the coalmines.

St. Andrew's Ambulance Association
EDINBURGH EXECUTIVE COMMITTEE

THE LOTHIANS MINE WORKERS' AMBULANCE LEAGUE
**MURRAY OF ELIBANK
CHALLENGE SHIELD COMPETITION**
SENIOR

Saturday, 12th April 1947
In St. Cuthbert's Halls, Edinburgh

PRACTICAL

1. The *squad* will treat No. 5 for a compound fracture of the right femur in the middle third, and for an internal compound fracture of the right fifth rib.

2. (a) *No.* 1 will treat No. 2 for a ruptured varicose vein of the left leg.

(b) *No.* 3 will treat No. 4 for a compound fracture of the left clavicle.

(c) *No.* 5 will treat No. 1 who is found strangled.

(d) *No.* 2 will treat No. 3 for a crushed right foot involving fractures of bones.

(e) *No.* 4 will treat No. 5 for a fracture of the right patella.

A. T. B. DICKSON, M.B., Ch.B.,
Arbiter.

About autumn of that year the foreman asked me if I was interested in joining the Colliery first aid classes held in the Band Hall. This was a few yards down from the White Gates in Newtongrange. I agreed to go along and find out if I would like it. I met him there one evening and he introduced me to everyone in the class. I was the youngest there and felt a bit out of place to start with but they soon got me involved. Some of the members were practising for first aid mining competitions. I watched for about an hour and I was then asked if I would like to help them by acting as their casualty. I found it very interesting and enjoyable. On the third week I was asked if I would be interested enough to join one of the teams as they were a member short. I said that I would give it a try. There were two teams, a senior team who were the experienced members and the junior team made up of first aiders who hadn't competed in a first aid competition before. I soon learned that being a member of a first aid team wasn't just turning up on class night. It was a lot of hard work studying and practising and very time consuming.

We practised as two separate teams. We often competed against each other on practice night. Other than meeting on class nights in the Band Hall we would also meet two or three extra nights elsewhere to practice for the competitions. The other nights would be held in the Ambulance Room and other parts of the pit- head. We would also meet in the Engineering Workshops where we would have special training in the treatment, rescuing and carrying of casualties. One evening we practiced in the Power House amongst the Electric Motors. I remember it was very noisy and that everything was clean and tidy. The motors were shining. Lily's Uncle Matt Henshaw worked there after he recovered from an accident at the coal face in the Lady Victoria. When the others had left, I stayed behind to have a chat and to keep him company for a while. I found it all a worthwhile experience. The two teams were known as Newbattle Collieries First Aid Teams.

The teams were as follows:
Senior Team: Alex Weston, Captain   Junior Team: Harry Atkins, Captain
                                                         Norman Anderson
              David Weston   Charles Armstrong
              John Knight   George Ralston
              Walter Haldane   Edward Miller
              James Lockhart

After many weeks of practice the day of the competition arrived and everyone was very nervous. Those of us who hadn't entered a competition before didn't know what to expect. The competition was held on the 12th of April 1947. The senior team was competing for the Elibank Challenge Shield for Lothian Mineworkers. On the same day the junior team were competing for the Wilson Trophy. Each team had to compete in a practical team test and an individual test where each member was given an incident to deal with and each team member had a question paper on first aid. I found it a very nervous but worthwhile experience. At the end of the competition both teams had an excellent result. The senior team were winners of their competition, the Elibank Shield and the junior team were also winners of their competition, the Wilson Trophy. We were all very excited when the results were announced and thrilled when both teams went on to the stage to receive the trophies.

> **AMBULANCE COMPETITION**
>
> The annual competition of the Lothians Mineworkers' Ambulance League was held in Edinburgh on Saturday. Lord Balfour, the chairman of the Scottish Division of the National Coal Board, presented the prizes.
>
> Results:—Individual competition—1, John Howie, Arniston (162 marks out of 200); 2, George Davidson, Niddrie (161); 3 (equal), James Miffen, Riddochhill, and David Weston, Lady Victoria (158). Special prizes—Oral—1, William Howat, Mid Breich (87 out of 100); 2, George Davidson, Niddrie (86). Practical—1, James Miffen, Riddochhill (82); 2, David Weston, Lady Victoria (81).
>
> Wilson Cup for junior teams—1, Lady Victoria (H. Atkins, E. Miller, C. Armstrong, N. Anderson, G. Ralston) (218 marks out of 300); 2, Niddrie (A. Malcolm, J. Hollerin, J. R. Smith, J. Bell, M. Lynch) (214); 3, Hopetoun Collieries (R. Meikle, R. Sneddon, J. Walker, F. M'Queen, R. Newton) (197). Special prizes—Oral—Niddrie (91 out of 100). Practical—Lady Victoria (66).
>
> Marquis of Elibank Shield for senior teams—1, Lady Victoria (Alex. Weston, David Weston, James Lockbart, W. Haldane, John Knight) (259 out of 300); 2, Arniston (J. Howie, William Davidson, M. Weir, G. Stevenson, G. Brunton) (233); 3, Foulshiels (J. Irving, Ben Stankiatis, J. Smellie, Archibald Pratt, J. Murray) (226). Special prizes—Oral—Lady Victoria (98 out of 100). Practical—Lady Victoria (81).

The next competition we entered was the Edinburgh and District Shield. As the senior team had won this competition the previous year the rules stated that before they could enter they must make at least three changes in the team. The other problem was that as the junior team had won the Wilson Trophy we were no longer classed as juniors. To solve the problem it was decided to have two senior teams, and enter both in the Edinburgh & District Shield. The teams were known as Newbattle No.1. & No.2. Three members from No.1.team were transferred into No.2 team and three members from No. 2 team into No.1.

The teams were as follows:

No 1:   Alex Weston   No 2:   John Knight
        David Weston   James Lockhart
        Walter Haldane   Harry Atkins
        Charles Armstrong   Norman Anderson
        Edward Millar   George Ralston

My Surname - Ralston would sometimes be spelt the same as the local G.P. Dr. Roulston.

NEWBATTLE

AMBULANCE SECTION. — A notable success was gained by the Newbattle section of the St Andrew's Ambulance Association at the annual ambulance competition for the East of Scotland Challenge Shield at Tollcross School, Edinburgh, on Saturday, when the local team were runners-up to Cowdenbeath, who won the trophy. The competition is open to all ambulance teams in the East of Scotland, and the first two winning teams qualify to compete in the competition for the President's Cup in Glasgow, with similar winners of other area competitions throughout Scotland. The local section won the Challenge Shield last year, but, according to the competition rules, the winning team, in a succeeding competition, must show at least three changes in the team personnel. It is therefore, a highly gratifying performance for the section to have two successive years qualified to compete in the national competition. This year's successful team, who are to be congratulated on their signal success, comprise Messrs John Knight (captain), and James Lockhart, who were members of last year's trophy-winning team, and Harry Atkins, Norman Anderson, and George Roulston. Hopes are high in the section that further ambulance successes will be secured in forthcoming competitions.

NEWTONGRANGE

AMBULANCE COMPETITION.— In the Midlothian Mineworkers' Ambulance League competition for the Elibank Trophy, held under the auspices of the St. Andrew's Ambulance Association in Edinburgh on Saturday, Lady Victoria Pit team gained the premier award and the special wards for the highest points in the oral and practical competitions. The winning team were—Alex. Weston (captain), David Weston, John Knight, Walter Haldane, and James Lockhart, who recently representing Newhill, won the St. Andrew's Ambulance Competition in Edinburgh and were runners up in Glasgow. The Lady Victoria Pit junior team, comprising Harry Atkins (captain), Norman Anderson, Charles Armstrong, George Roulston, and Edward Miller, gained the Wilson Trophy and special award for the highest points in practical work. The individual championship was won by John Howie, Arniston Colliery; David Weston and John Knight, Lady Victoria, secured third and fourth place respectively in the same competition. By their victory, Lady Victoria team qualify to compete for the President's Cup in Glasgow next month. The success by both senior and junior teams has created general satisfaction in the village.

The day of our second competition arrived and like before we were all very nervous. Everyone gave his best. When the results were given out we were all delighted to learn that the team I was in, (No. 2) were second to Cowdenbeath Co-op. We had lost by only 4 ½ marks. We were also overjoyed to learn that we had beaten Waverley Station one of the top teams in the district. Fifteen teams competed in the competition. As a result of our success both Newbattle teams qualified to take part in the Presidents Cup, which was held in Glasgow. Neither of the teams was successful in Glasgow but I enjoyed the experience especially as we were competing against the top First Aid teams in Scotland.

First aid knowledge and training is very important in the mining industry and is encouraged by colliery management in every part of the country. I found that I was a better person as a result of the training I received. It gave me a lot of confidence when dealing with an accident. The training I received as a member of St. Andrews Ambulance and as a first aid team member stood me in good stead when I returned to Corby and joined the St. John Ambulance Brigade. I also found that studying first aid gave me something to do in the evenings and helped pass the time. There wasn't much to do in the hostel after work. I noticed that many of the other Bevin Boys would just sit around most nights. I was fortunate to have an interest and through attending classes I made many friends in and around Newtongrange.

Lily's Mum (front left) and friends

Lily, Joan and Joan's friend

John, Lily and Alan at back door (1945/46)

Lily's Dad with Lily holding a baby

Lily in the park

Attending a Road Accident

The first occasion when I had to use my first aid knowledge was on a visit to my Auntie Annie's in Newarthill. I was travelling on a bus along the Holytown Newhouse Road in Lanarkshire when I heard a screech of brakes and then a crash. I got off the bus to find out what had happened and to help if necessary. When I got off the bus I saw that a black Rolls Royce had hit a telegraph pole. The side of the car was open and a woman lying on the ground. The driver sitting behind the wheel had injured both arms.

I treated the passenger lying on the road who appeared to have a fractured femur. I learned later that she was Lady Roberton the wife of Sir Hugh Roberton Conductor of the Glasgow Orpheus Choir. He told me he wasn't injured and that he was on his way to give a concert in the Usher Hall in Edinburgh. He was very concerned that the organisers of the concert should know about the accident and asked if someone would contact them. Two of the other injured passengers were taken to a house nearby. The police and ambulance arrived soon afterwards.

Orpheus Party in Car Crash

LADY Roberton, wife of Sir Hugh Roberton, conductor of the Orpheus Choir, who was injured in a car crash near Newhouse, Lanarkshire. yesterday, was stated at Glasgow Royal Infirmary to-day to be "fairly comfortable."

One of the Orpheus Choir secretaries, Mr Alexander Christie, 127 Broomhill Drive, Glasgow, was also detained in the infirmary suffering from arm and knee injuries. His condition is "fairly comfortable."

Sir Hugh, Mrs Sandison (Lady Roberton's sister), and Mr Joseph Jackson, 49 Bearford Hillington, driver of the allowed home after

Meeting the Union

One morning when I arrived at work Willie Shaw told me that we were to receive a twelve-shilling and sixpence [62p] increase in our wages. This was a pleasant surprise as I was still finding it difficult to make ends meet. Friday couldn't come quick enough as I was looking forward to collecting my wages but when I received them there was no increase. As I couldn't understand the reason for this I asked to see the Manager of the wages office. When I spoke to him he told me the Union had decided that the increase was only being paid to union members. As I wasn't a member I would not be entitled to the increase.

Next morning at work I had a talk with my foreman about it. He told me that he wasn't aware of this decision but would try to arrange for me to see the Colliery Manager on the Monday. It was arranged that I should see him when I finished work. When we met I told him how upset I was, saying that as I was directed to work in the coalmines as a Bevin Boy, I felt that it was very unfair not to be receiving the rate for the job. He seemed very sympathetic but was sorry he couldn't help me as it was a union decision. He asked if I would like to meet the local union representative and talk to him about it. I said yes and a meeting was arranged. The shop steward came to see me at the hostel where I put forward my case. He listened but there was nothing he was prepared to do for me unless I joined the union. I asked him what it would cost me and he told me that I would have to pay an entrance fee plus weekly membership contributions. I said I couldn't afford it. Before leaving he told me to think it over.

I did think it over and decided to write to the head office in Edinburgh explaining my case. I addressed my letter to The President of the Miners union. I didn't know what to expect. Perhaps I would receive a letter explaining their decision not to pay me. A few days later at the end of my shift I called at the office in the hostel to see if there was any mail. The manager met me and told me I had a visitor. I was surprised when the visitor introduced himself. He was one of the top union officials from Head Office in Edinburgh. The local shop steward was also there.

We were allowed to hold our meeting in the reading room, as it was vacant. I thanked him for taking the time to come to see me. He said that he had read my letter with interest and wanted to talk to me about it. I told him what I had told the Shop Steward that as a Bevin Boy, I was conscripted against my wishes to work in the coalmines and was of the opinion that I was entitled to the rate for the job. A miner had been able to be released to the coalface. This person would have been paid a higher rate for working on the haulage when I took over from him. I also explained that all the Bevin Boys were, like me, finding it difficult to make ends meet on the wages we were receiving. Perhaps I was receiving a lower rate of pay as I was less than 21 years of age?

He listened to what I had to say and we also discussed other matters. He mentioned that a number of miners were unhappy that Bevin Boys hadn't joined the Miners' Union and were getting the benefits that they had fought for. I told him that I didn't think we were getting any benefits other than what we felt we were entitled to as Bevin Boys.

I thanked him again for coming to see me. It showed that the Union was interested in us. At the end of the meeting his final decision was that the Union would waive the membership entrance fee but to receive the increase I would have to join the union and pay my weekly contributions. I had no choice but to accept. I couldn't afford to turn down the offer, as I needed the extra money. At the end of our meeting I felt he was fair and our meeting was worthwhile. I said that I hoped he understood more about the Bevin Boys' feelings about being called up to work in the pits and our struggle to make ends meet.

The final outcome of the meeting was that I received my twelve shillings and sixpence [62p] increase. I don't remember if I received any back money for the weeks I wasn't paid the increase. I asked the hostel manager if he would put a notice on the board to tell the other Bevin Boys about the outcome of the meeting. My main reason for mentioning this is that in all the time I worked in the coalmines I had never met anyone from the Union. I had the feeling that the Miners Union wasn't in agreement with the Bevin Scheme and to us being conscripted to work in the coalmines.

Looking back, it might have helped if a Union Official from Edinburgh had come to the hostel to meet us to learn about our problems. I also felt, like many other Bevin Boys that the government wanted to forget about us once we had become the responsibility of the Coal Owners. In other words, we were on our own. Later, when I thought about the unions decision not to pay us the increase, I wondered if it was their way of making the Bevin Boys join the union because to my knowledge very few, if any of the Bevin Boys living in the hostel were union members. If the same rule applied to all the other Bevin Boys in the country the union would have 42,000 new members.

My first visit to a coal face

It was time for my first visit to the coalface but I kept putting it off. I had often heard about the poor conditions the men worked under. However, the foreman thought that as the section first aider I should become familiar with the coalface at

Coalface

Trenchs and its workings in case I was called to an accident there. He arranged for me to visit with the fireman. The day arrived for my visit. Before leaving we went round the corner to clear it with 'Big Harry' the engine driver and Charlie Dickson who was responsible for that part of the dook. It was also Charlie's job to fasten the rope onto the empty hutches before sending them down to the coal face. When they said it was safe we left to walk down the steep incline. The fireman told me to take it steady on the way down, as the road was very steep and slippery in places where the water had been dripping from the roof. When we arrived at the bottom, I gave the pre-arranged signal to the engine driver by pressing the wires together to ring the bell three times to let them know that we had reached the bottom safe and sound.

From there we went along another road towards the coalface. As we got near I saw a lot of dust and could hardly hear for the noise. The dust and the noise were coming from the coal conveyor where a local lad about my age was working. I had seen him before on his way to and from work but I didn't know until then what his job was. He was covered from top to bottom in coal dust coming off the conveyor. He was as black as the ace of spades. I remember thinking that I wondered what his lungs would be like in a few years time. The noise wouldn't help his hearing either. Ear defenders were not issued in those days. I also remember how pleased I was not to be doing his job. All day and every day he would be pushing empty hutches under the conveyor to be filled with coal and then removing them. The full hutches would be sent up the dook to me to take out to the main haulage and sent to the pit bottom. I covered my mouth with my hand as we walked through the dust. I could see more dust in front of me and hear a lot of noise coming from the coalface.

The miners shovelling the coal onto the conveyors caused the dust and the noise was from what the miners called pans. These were flat pieces of metal bent up to prevent the coal that the miners were shovelling onto the conveyors from falling off the side. Suddenly everything went quiet, the dust settled and I could see more clearly from the lights of our lamps. It was what they called piece time, a 20 minutes break for the miners to eat their sandwiches. They would also have a drink of water or tea depending on their choice. Afterwards some of them would have a chew of tobacco. There was nowhere and no time for them to wash their hands before eating. I knew the men by this time and one after the other asked me if I would like a job at the coal face. You can guess my answer.

The coalface was about 3 feet 6 inches to 4 feet thick. I had to keep down low as I made my way along. Not being familiar with the conditions in the section I kept hitting my head on the roof. Fortunately I was wearing my safety helmet but each time it happened I felt a jarring pain at the back of my neck. This happened when I was trying to dodge my way around the pit props, sometimes called trees. They were made of pieces of round timber props inside seamless steel tubes similar to those we made in the Tube Works in Corby. They were used to hold in position 6 foot corrugated steel straps to help support the roof while the miners were working there.

All too soon the 20 minutes break was over and it was back to work for the miners. The noise started up again and the dust was once again flying everywhere. I had seen enough for my first visit and thought it was time for me to leave and get back to my own job. As the fireman had to remain at the coalface he arranged for Charlie Dickson to meet me at the bottom of the dook and look after me on my way back. I remember thinking that men should never have to work under such conditions. That is still my opinion. I made a number of visits to that section later, each time having to walk further as the coalface advanced.

Vesting Day/Nationalisation

1st January 1947 was the day when the Coal Industry was nationalised. We were told that it would be owned by the people and run on their behalf by the National Coal Board. This was the day the miners and their families had been looking forward to for as long as they could remember. The Day they hoped would be the beginning of an improvement in the working conditions of the miners and a better relationship with Management. I heard a number of complaints when it was learned that the same managers would still run the Coal Industry. I am certain that the miners were very disappointed at this decision by the Government. However, it did not stop the Celebrations that took place all over the Country which were in addition to the usual New Year parties that were taking place in the homes of every town and mining village.

When we returned to work, everyone seemed to be more cheerful in the early days. The miners were looking forward to better working conditions and a better future for themselves and their families. I think perhaps every one of us expected things to improve quickly but we soon realised that this was not going to happen. It would take time and we would just have to be patient. One of the earliest improvements that I do remember was when we went on the Five-Day Week. It meant that when we worked five days, we would be paid six, the extra day would be classed as a bonus shift. If we lost a day during the week it meant we also lost the bonus shift. We were still expected to work on the Saturday as usual for which we were paid an extra shift. This new system was very welcome to me as it helped my financial situation a great deal as it did all the other Bevin Boys.

Robert's Injury

It was at the end of one of my late shift early in October when my girl friend Lily Walton was waiting for me outside the pit gates. I know when I saw her that something was wrong. I wasn't prepared for the bad news. She told me that her sister Joan had phoned her at work in Edinburgh. Joan told Lily that she had read in the evening paper that my twin brother Robert and two of his army friends had been attacked by a Malayan on the train while travelling to Singapore. They were on their way home to be de-mobbed. Sadly his two friends died from their injuries. Robert was taken to the hospital in Kuala Lumpar to be treated for his injuries. He was on the danger list for a few weeks.

After a few days, the foreman could see that I was still worried and my mind wasn't on my work. He was concerned that I might have another accident and suggested that I take a few days compassionate leave. He said that he would make the necessary arrangements with the office. I was very grateful for his kindness and understanding and thanked him very much. I checked out of the Hostel explaining the situation to the office girls. They understood and told me not to worry about my room and bed. My accommodation would still be there when I returned.

I caught the evening train from Edinburgh and arrived in Corby next morning. My father was surprised and pleased to see me. He didn't know I was coming home. We didn't have a phone in those days. I was home for about a week when a Policeman arrived at the door. We expected the worst but it was good news. The Police had been asked by the Army to tell us that Robert had been taken off the danger list and was on the road to recovery.

I caught the train back to Newtongrange next morning feeling much better. I booked back into the hostel in the evening ready to start back to work next morning. When I reported for work in the morning, the foreman and my work mates were delighted with the good news and pleased to see me back. This confirmed what I already know, that I had made many good friends during my years as a Bevin Boy and would always remember their kindness.

The Roof Fall

One of the days I shall always remember most while serving as a Bevin Boy and also a reminder of just how dangerous it was working in the pits, was one morning when the foreman and I escaped a roof fall. It was a day like every other day except that I had decided to start work a bit early. The miners at the coalface had run out of empty hutches and needed them for the start of the shift. I had just taken my second rake of empty hutches inside the mine ready for the men starting work. I was on my way out with full hutches when I met the foreman on the way in to do his rounds. I pressed the two wires together once to signal Bob Scott the engine driver to stop the haulage rope.

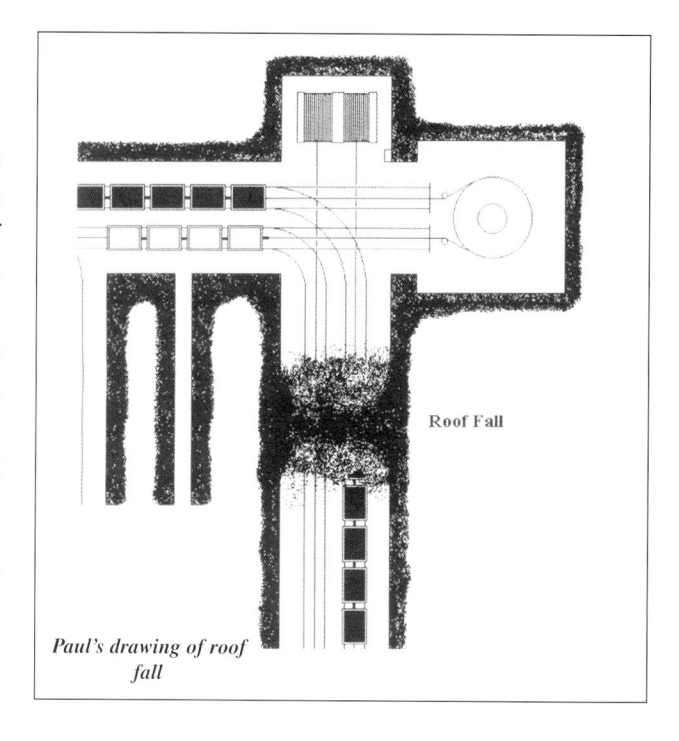

Paul's drawing of roof fall

This was the first time that morning the foreman and I had time for a chat. Every morning he would ask me how the job was going and if I had any problems. He was pleased when I told him that I had started early and taken in two lots of empties. After a few minutes he said that he would have to go and just before he left I pressed the two wires together to restart the haulage rope. The hutches moved a few inches and stopped suddenly. I could see that the rope was still moving and being pulled through the clip. I couldn't understand what was happening. Before I had the chance to stop the haulage there was a sudden rumbling sound, the roof was coming down. Rocks and dust was falling around our feet. The fall was just where we had both been standing seconds earlier. I ran out towards the main haulage, as I didn't know what else to do or how much of the roof was coming down. When I reached the main haulage I stopped and looked back to where the roof had come down. When I thought it was safe I went back to see what had happened.

When I got there I shouted the foreman's name a few times but there was no answer. My first thought was that he was buried underneath the fall. Just then, to my relief, I saw a flicker of light shining through a small gap and it was moving. Then I heard him shout my name. He was all right. It was a relief for both of us. The fall had been so sudden and so close that both of us thought the other was buried underneath. We had a narrow escape. We both had such a fright. I thought once again my luck has held.

By this time Bob Scott the engine driver was standing beside me. When he saw me running down towards the main haulage he new something was wrong and stopped the haulage. He was amazed when he saw the fall. He accompanied me to the engine room where we had to sit down for a few minutes. Then we both went back to the roof fall to see if we could help in any way but there was nothing we could do from this side. By this time Willie Shaw my other work mate had arrived he jokingly asked what we had been up to. I remembered later that this was where the water had been dripping from and perhaps had loosened the earth above

The foreman made arrangements from the inside to have the fall cleared, as he was unable to get through to where I was. I expect he arranged for the miners to come up from the coalface to help clear the rubble. It was fortunate that there were plenty of empty hutches inside for them to make use of. As soon as there was enough rubble cleared to allow the foreman to squeeze through he came down to the engine room to see how I was feeling. He could see that I was a bit shaken by this time. As there was nothing I could do until the fall was cleared he suggested that I should go home early. I told him that I would rather wait in the engine room for a while and talk to Bob Scott and Willie Shaw. He said that was fine by him if it would make me feel better. I told him I had got such a fright that if I went back to the Hostel I might not want to come back to work.

Just before lunch time Jimmy Sharpe the fitter and Piper Mc.Queen the rope splicer arrived. They couldn't get through to go any further so they joined us for lunch. After a while, to pass the time, I walked out to see Bill Currie and his assistants Bobby Dyer and Pete Dickson and helped them send the full hutches from the Splint section to the pit bottom. I thought it would take my mind off what happened.

Quicker than I expected it was time to make our way up to the pit bottom. The fall was still not cleared when I left. Thinking about it later, I always walked alongside the first hutch on the way out and if I hadn't met the Foreman that morning I might have been directly under the fall. Again I believe my guardian angel was with me.

Next morning when I arrived back to work everything was cleared and empties waiting for me to take inside the mine. I thought that I would be nervous starting back to work after the fright I had but to my surprise I was fine. When the foreman asked me how I was feeling I said all right and that I felt better having stayed on afterwards talking to my mates. It was better than going back to the hostel where I would be on my own and worrying about it. The only thing that worried me was the large hole in the roof left after the fall. Every time I reached it I would hurry past. It was a few days before I had the courage to stop and shine my lamp up into the hole. All I could see was a black space as far as the light could show. There had been quite a fall.

I asked the foreman if he knew what had caused it. He told me that the first hutch had been damaged earlier making it stick out at one of the corners. This was what had caught on the arched girder moving it enough to loosen the roof and causing it to come down. He told me that as an extra precaution he had the rails moved a few inches further away from the wall to prevent the same thing happening again. I mentioned to the foreman a few days later that I was worried about pieces of loose materials falling down where the hole was. He arranged for someone to put a piece of sheet metal across. This solved the problem.

The Day the Cage Dropped

They say things happen in threes. Well this was my third and most frightening experience while working in the coalmines. This was the day I thought would be my last. It happened on a Saturday at the end of the shift. My work mate Willie Shaw and I made our way up to the pit bottom as usual ready to go home. The cage reached the bottom of the shaft a few minutes after we arrived. There were more miners than usual waiting to get on the cage and everyone seemed to be in a hurry. When I remarked about this I was told that it was a big day for the village as the local football team, Newtongrange Star, (known affectionately as 'The Star') were playing in an important Cup Match that day. Everyone was in a hurry to get home early to get ready to go and watch them.

I mentioned earlier that the cage held about 50 men but there seemed to be more than usual getting on the cage this time. No sooner had I got on the cage and it was full. We were on our way up the shaft to the pithead. The cage seemed to be travelling faster than usual which was understandable under the circumstances. I could see daylight as we neared the top of the shaft. Without warning, the cage suddenly dropped. It seemed to be falling so fast we all thought the rope had broken. No one spoke except Willie Shaw who said what we were all thinking. His words were something like, well lads, this is it. There was no panic. We were all waiting for something to happen, not knowing what, everyone thinking their own thoughts.

I remember thinking there is too many men on this cage and about my family back home. How will they feel when they hear about the accident? I don't know how far the cage dropped but it seemed a long way to me. Just as suddenly we felt the cage slowing down and then stopping. I could not believe it. When we started moving upwards again everyone gave a sigh of relief. What a wonderful feeling it was. I can't describe how I felt except that I was shaking. I am sure everyone felt the same as I did.

Still no one spoke as we got off the cage at the pithead. Not even when we handed in our lamp and token. We were all quiet. Everyone was black with coal dust as usual but I am sure their faces were white underneath with the shock we just had. When I reached my hut there was no one to talk to. My roommates were still at work. I sat on my bed for a few minutes to get my thoughts together before going for a shower. After getting dressed I lay on my bed for a while before going to the canteen for lunch. I didn't enjoy it. I wasn't very hungry. I decided not to go to my grandparents that weekend.

I needed to relax so I phoned Lily my girl friend who was working in Houlisons a Millinery shop on Lothian Road Edinburgh. I asked her if I could meet her when she finished work. She asked me if I would call and tell her mother that she wouldn't be home till later. I had met her mother earlier and she was a lovely person. I liked her from the first time we met and we got on well together.

The girls in the shop knew me by this time and told Lily when they saw me waiting outside. When she finished work we walked down Lothian Road to Princes Street Gardens where we sat on one of the seats for a while. It was while we were sitting on the seat I told her what happened at work and that I wanted to see her and spend a bit of time with her in Edinburgh.

From there we went to our favourite restaurant the "Brown Derby" on Princes Street. The entrance was by a side street. When we went up the stairs to the restaurant I was pleased to see that our favourite table was vacant. It was beside a window looking down to Princes Street where I always enjoyed the view. We could watch the crowds below, some hurrying along and others walking at their leisure and looking in the shop windows. Many of those walking along the street enjoying the scenery were service men and women of various Nationalities including Americans, Canadians, and Polish.

There were also many British servicemen and women visiting the Capital. As there was a Scottish Regiment based in Edinburgh they were always prominent. From where we were sitting we could see the Castle up on the hill and watch everyone enjoying themselves in the famous Princes Street gardens. Some people would be sitting on the seats or on the grass when the weather was nice. On many occasions a band would be playing in the Bandstand and the visitors would enjoy themselves listening to the music while others were dancing. We could also see Scott's Monument. I remember the first

"Dad" Peter Ralston
Drummer in Stewarts & Lloyds Pipeband

time I climbed the steps to the top. The view was wonderful looking along Princes Street. We had a good view of the gardens and the Castle. We could see for miles around Edinburgh in every direction.

On other visits to Edinburgh later, if I had enough energy, I would climb to the top of Arthurs Seat for yet another view of the city. Each one would be a bit different but just as enjoyable. On one of my visits to Edinburgh I went to a photographer's and had my photo taken in Highland Dress to send home to my dad. I mentioned earlier that he played in a Pipe Band in Corby. I thought I would surprise

Myself in Highland Dress
Taken in Edinburgh

him. Later that day Lily and I went to the cinema at the top of Lothian Road a few yards up from the shop. I don't remember the name of the picture we went to see but I do remember that I enjoyed my day very much. It helped me relax. We were a bit late getting home but it didn't matter, as we didn't have to work next day.

I slept better than I expected on the Saturday night, perhaps because I was more relaxed. However, I didn't sleep very well on the Sunday night. I was worried about going down the cage again on the Monday morning. As I was stepping onto the cage I felt a bit nervous but when it reached the pit bottom safely I was relieved. When I arrived at my job in the morning I told Dave Young the foreman what had happened and asked him if he had any idea what had caused the cage to drop so suddenly. He didn't know anything about it but the only explanation he could give was that when the cage is travelling too fast and it gets near the surface, automatic brakes take over to prevent the cage going over the big wheels at the top. During the delay in the brakes taking affect, the cage had dropped giving us the impression the rope had broken. It is an unpleasant sensation that I will always remember. I forget the result of the Star's football match.

The winter of 1946/47

The winter of 1946/47 was the worst for many years. Everyone seemed to be caught out by the sudden change in the weather. There were blinding snowstorms and deep snowdrifts all over the country. When the thaw came at the end of March there were floods everywhere. I specially remember the first night of the snowstorm in 1946. As we didn't have any heating in the hostel we all shivered unable to sleep much because of the cold. Those of us who lived in the hostel were also caught out by the sudden change in the weather. It seemed colder than usual. I lay awake for ages before getting off to sleep. I felt that I had just dropped off to sleep when the caretaker came round in the morning with his usual, 'Wakey, Wakey, First Call'! to waken us for work. I tried to pull the blankets over my head but they were tucked too tightly under the mattress to try and keep my feet warm but they were still cold.

Although it was cold in bed we didn't feel like getting out of it to get ready for work. Finally, I jumped out of bed and quickly got dressed for work, dashed down to the washroom for a quick wash with hot water. It felt good. I then made my way to the canteen for breakfast. When I got outside the huts, I was surprised at the amount of snow that had fallen during the night. Everywhere was covered and it was very deep. I had to take care walking to the canteen. When I arrived there it was nice and warm.

I went into the kitchen, collected my breakfast and sat down beside the others. We complained to each other about the weather and how cold it was in the huts. I enjoyed the breakfast that morning. It was lovely and warm, the tea was nice and hot and I had an extra cup. I tucked into the usual breakfast, porridge, sausage and egg, and fried bread. I had an extra helping of toast to pass the time. I wanted to sit longer in the warm but I had to make a move, as I still had to collect my sandwiches and fill my flask. This was one of the times I decided to take tea, black with sugar even although it would be cold when I was having my break. Cold black tea is quite a pleasant drink. Many miners took it to work. I had to hurry, as I didn't want to risk missing the last cage down the pit. The snow was too deep to go out the side door of the dining room. I had to go back the way I had come and out the main road.

With a struggle I waded through the deep snow. It had drifted almost to the top of the 4 foot wall that surrounded the hostel. I finally reached the pit office and collected my tokens and lamp. I then made my way up the slippery steps to the cage. When I arrived at the pithead there seemed to be fewer miners waiting to go down the pit that morning. I put it down to the heavy snowfall. I learned later that some miners were unable to get to work that day. The miners, who lived outside the village and depended on public transport, were specially affected. It was mostly those of us who lived nearby and able to walk to work that turned up. We didn't have the early warning forecasts then that we have now.

All during the winter months there was a big shortage of coal all over the country. The railways were badly affected by the snow and the frost. The coal that was lying at the Railway Sidings couldn't be moved. Industry, homes and even the armed forces camps suffered from lack of coal. Many of the service men, and women were sent home on special leave because they were unable to get enough coal through to heat the camps.

The Bevin Boys however had to put up with the cold and stay in the hostel and like the miners, go to work. As I mentioned earlier, the worst time was in bed at night. We didn't have pyjamas to wear. We couldn't afford the clothing coupons, or have the money to buy them. Like most of the other lads, I had to wear the Long Johns and socks I bought for work to try and keep warm. To get better use of my blankets I had to fold them over to make a sleeping bag and crawl into it from the top. This helped a bit but it was still cold, especially when I got out of bed in the mornings. As soon as I put my feet onto the floor the cold went straight through me. I would make a quick dash for a wash before changing for work.

For the first few weeks those of us in the hostel went out as little as possible. After work we would spend most of our time in the lounge, reading room or the games room, where it was warmer. As the weather improved, I would sometimes make my way as far as the pictures house and then make my way to the Miners' Welfare for a game of billiards. I would spend some time in the reading room where there were always plenty of daily papers and magazines to read. When the road conditions improved I went to Dalkeith, the buses were more comfortable then.

I remember when I first arrived in Newtongrange, travelling on some of the buses was very uncomfortable. The seats were made of wood, two and a half inch by three quarter inch pieces of timber, similar to garden seats. These were Special buses for taking miners to and from work. I expect some passengers had complained about getting their clothes dirty from the coal dust off the miner's clothes. The miners weren't really to blame as very few pits in the area had baths at that time. Many of the miners had to travel to and from work on the bus, some like my mate Charlie Dickson who had to travel as far as Edinburgh still wearing the clothes they worked in. I believe it was sometime in 1947 when we had a new Manager in the Hostel. He was a retired army officer who, I understood had been serving in India. I found him a good manager and very fair to his staff and those of us living in the hostel. However one of the first decisions he made didn't go down very well with some of the lads in the hostel. He decided that each of us would look after our own mug and cutlery. This meant that we had to wash them after each meal and carry them back and forth to the canteen. The committee, who represented the Bevin Boys, called a meeting to discuss the matter. It was decided that we were not in agreement and informed the manager of our decision.

The committee notified one of the Daily Newspapers in Edinburgh who sent out a reporter and a photographer to meet us. We met outside the entrance of the hostel, each of us carrying our mug. The photographer set up his camera and we walked to the middle of the road about three yards from the stone wall that surrounded the hostel. When the photographer was ready we threw our mugs against the wall, where they smashed. That was our protest. As soon as my mug hit the wall I thought, what a stupid thing to do. It didn't do us any good. The manager stood by his decision. We had to buy another mug. When I thought about it afterwards, I felt that the manager was right. I would rather wash and carry my own mug and cutlery. At least I knew that it would always be clean.

It taught me a lesson, to think for myself and to make up my own mind.

Cosgroves

I believe it was sometime during 1947 when a new coalface was opened in Carrington section. This one was called Cosgrove's after the Contractor who was in charge of the coalface and the men who would be working there. If my memory serves me right the Fireman's name was Jim Peacock. I was surprised about this new development as I didn't know anything about a new coalface being planned until I arrived one morning and found men I hadn't seen before working behind the large wooden doors at the end of Whitehill Mine and taking measurements. When I asked the Fireman what they were doing he told me that a new coalface was being opened beyond the doors.

Within a few days the doors had been removed and progress was being made to develop the site. Each morning when I arrived for work there were flat bogies at the end of the mine loaded with rails, sleepers, pit props, or trees as they were sometimes called. There would also be other metal supports for the haulage road leading to the coalface and any other equipment required by the miners who would be working there. Everything that was needed would be brought down the pit and sent to the new section after we had gone home at the end of our shift. This was to prevent production being interrupted during the day shift. Sooner than I had expected the new coalface was ready for production and miners taken on to work there.

Gradually work increased and in a matter of weeks production had increased so much that my work had almost doubled and I was finding it difficult to keep both sections supplied with empty hutches and also taking the full ones out to the main haulage to be sent up to the pit bottom. On most days I had to work late to make sure there were enough empties ready for the coalface workers starting work in the morning. The main haulage would run late to clear the full hutches and keep me supplied with empties for the next morning.

I was working long hours and although the extra money came in handy it was getting too much for me. I mentioned this to the foreman. A few days later he asked me if I would consider working what was called the Ham & Egg Shift. He explained that I would work from 9 a.m. until 5 p.m. The shift was given that name because anyone working those hours would be able to have time for a ham & egg breakfast. Not that we were allowed many eggs, even in 1947. Someone from the coalface covered my job until I arrived at 9 a.m. After covering the shift for about two months I asked the foreman if I could work it every second week, as it was sometimes 7 or 8 o,clock some evenings before I got back from the pit and he agreed to this. I know I was earning extra money but by the time I was arriving back at the hostel, showered, changed and had something to eat it was time for bed. I wasn't getting much extra sleep starting at 9 a.m. as I was wakened on the early morning call.

One of the reasons for the increased production of coal in 1947 was there was a good feeling amongst the miners after Nationalisation and at the same time the Government had asked the miners to increase coal production. There was a big demand for power by the factories changing over to peacetime production. The miners in the Lady Victoria were certainly pulling their weight at this time. They were regularly breaking records and if might give myself a pat on the back, I was also playing my part. I couldn't do anything else as everyone worked as a team, helping each other and perhaps without being aware of it at the time I felt part of that team.

Visit to Cosgroves Coal Face

One morning, when things were unusually quiet, Jim Peacock the Fireman thought that it was a good opportunity for me, as the section First Aider, to pay a visit to the new coalface and become familiar with the surroundings. On that particular morning he had arranged for one of the miners to accompany me to the coalface. He had already been in to check that everything was safe and everyone clear as he was making preparations for shot firing. When I had first heard Shot Firing mentioned I asked what it meant. I was given a brief explanation. I was told that holes were drilled at regular intervals in the coalface and an explosive then put in the hole then packed with clay. An electric wire was attached and led to a safe distance away from the coalface. Men were then posted at a safe distance as sentries to keep other miners away from the danger area. The Fireman would then detonate the charge from a safe distance.

On that particular morning he made certain that everyone was at a safe distance and someone looking after me. He then fired the shot. I heard the sudden noise and then the blast as the air rushed past. In no time all around us was filled with coal dust. What I remember most was the smell of the powder. I could taste it and the dust at the back of my throat for some time afterwards. The dust and powder soon cleared and after a safety check everyone went back to work. The fireman then arranged for someone to accompany me to the coalface. When I arrived there the miners were busy shovelling the coal onto the conveyor. I found everything familiar to what I had seen when I visited Trenchs section. When the fireman asked me if I had seen enough on this visit I said yes. He took me back to the alcove to fill in his report. He said it was quieter there and not too far away from the coalface if he was needed. When we returned I couldn't sit and talk about my visit as there were about a dozen full hutches ready to be taken out to the main haulage and there were no empties waiting to be sent to the coal face. As Cosgroves coalface was nearer than Trenchs I paid more visits.

The Accident at Cosgroves

One of my visits to Cosgroves was to treat someone who had an accident on the haulage road. I had just arrived inside the mine when someone came running up from the section saying there had been an accident and a man was injured. I collected the First Aid bag and asked him to bring the two blankets. I followed him to where the accident was and found a man lying between the rails of the haulage road. His job was the same as mine. I asked him what happened. He told me that while he was walking along in front of the hutches he hadn't noticed that the wire rope had been running between the joint in the rails. Suddenly without warning the rope sprung out just like a whip, hitting him on the leg. He managed to get clear before falling to the ground. He was in a lot of pain. I told him to lie still. When I examined his leg I diagnosed a fracture of the lower leg. I was pleased that there was no wound lessening the risk of infection from the coal dust. I gently immobilised the fracture using the splints and bandages from my First Aid bag. After covering him with one of the blankets to keep him warm he was ready to be taken to the pit bottom.

Having experienced an accident down the pit myself I knew how he was feeling and how uncomfortable he must be. I tried my best to re-assure him. I knew how long it would be before he reached the pithead. Fortunately there was an empty flat bogie in the section. We carefully lifted him onto the stretcher before lifting him onto the bogie. I covered him with the other blanket knowing how cold it is travelling on a bogie up the main haulage. It is a long slow journey to the pit bottom this way as the bogie is clipped onto the haulage rope, which doesn't travel very fast. However, I knew from experience that it would be the most comfortable way to travel.

By this time Dave Young the foreman had arrived from Trench's. I asked him if I could travel with the casualty to the pit bottom in case there should there be problems on the way. I also asked him if he would make arrangements for an ambulance to be waiting at the pithead to take him to hospital. After a long cold journey we reached the pit bottom where someone was waiting to accompany the casualty to the pithead where an ambulance was waiting. Unfortunately I don't remember his name, but I do remember he was Irish.

I am pleased to say it was the most serious accident that I had to deal with while I worked there, although I had quite a few minor wounds to treat. As there were no facilities for cleaning minor wounds iodine was often used to prevent infection. It wasn't very popular with the casualty as it stung quite a bit. I remember having to treat myself when I caught my thumb between the haulage clip and the hutch. My thumbnail was black and anyone who has had this type of injury will know how painful it is. I remembered when I worked at my previous job at Stewarts & Lloyds I had a similar injury. When I went to the Ambulance Room the nurse used a very small drill to make a small hole in my nail and released the blood. What a relief it was. I didn't have a drill in my first aid bag but what I did have were safety pins. I brushed the point of one of the safety pins with iodine and scratched my thumbnail with it until the blood was released from underneath. I then covered it with a plaster. It was such a relief when the pain had gone.

The day the sole came off my boot

When I was returning from one of my early visits to Cosgroves, I caught my boot underneath one of the sleepers holding the rails. They hadn't been long put down and hadn't settled. They were still lying on top of the floor of the mine and some were a bit uneven. When I pulled my foot out from under the sleeper I saw that the sole of my boot had come away from the uppers. I wondered what I was going to do. I still had more than half a shift to do. I went to my first aid box and took out a 2-inch roller bandage and wrapped it around my boot hoping it would hold it together. It did for a short while but I could see that it wasn't going to be very successful. It was near break time when the electrician arrived I asked him if he had any suggestions. He took out a roll of black tape and wrapped it around my boot. That was much better. He gave me the rest of the roll just in case I needed it. I did, but only once more before I left to walk up the haulage to the pit bottom.

When Dave Young the foreman arrived I told him what happened and that I would need a new pair of safety boots, he agreed. When I told him that I didn't have any coupons left he told me to go over to the Main Office at the end of my shift. He would make arrangements for me to see someone in one of the offices. When I reported there I was directed to an office on the right just inside the main entrance where I saw the clerk who worked there. I explained what had happened and told him that I needed a new pair of safety boots but I didn't have any coupons. He then told me that I couldn't have boots without them. I said that that would be all right with me but I won't be allowed to work down the pit unless I was wearing safety boots. I then made to walk out of the office.

I was bluffing. I wanted to give him the impression that I didn't care. He called me back to discuss it and ask if I was one of our Bevin Boy's. He then asked me where I came from and I told him Corby. He said he knew people who had moved to Corby from Airdrie and he then asked me where I lived before moving there. I told him a small village called Chapelhall about three miles from Airdrie. He said he thought he recognised the accent and said that that makes us practically neighbours. He then told me he lived in Airdrie before moving to Newtongrange.

We talked about the places we knew, the dance halls and the picture houses that we went to. I told him that I had worked in the Odeon Cinema before moving to Corby. We talked for some time. Before I left he said that under the circumstances he would make out a special case for me. I could have the boots and pay for them over a few weeks the money deducted from my wages.

My De-mob.

It is now nearly Springtime 1948. The war has been over nearly three years and like other Bevin Boys I have been working in the coalmines for more than three and a half years. We had received no information as to when or how we would be released from our National Service. I had read in the newspapers of service men being de-mobbed and wondered when it would be my turn. I learned later, again through the newspapers, that Bevin Boys would be released, or de-mobbed as it was called, by a code number similar to the army. Each of us was given a number depending on when we were called up for National Service. We would be released when the number was due. If I remember correctly my number was either 65 or 67 and I would be due for release at the end of May 1948.

Before receiving my Code Number I had a letter from The National Coal Board headed 'To Ballottees, Optants and Volunteers'. We thank you for your services to the Coal Mining Industry and appreciate very much the good work you have done. You have become somewhat experienced by now and we shall be sorry to lose your services. You came to us at a time of great stress and strain, the need for coal and the manpower is as great, if not greater, than when you came to us. We are therefore appealing to you to consider favourably, remaining with us for a further temporary period to help tide us over the immediate crisis. We can definitely promise you will not prejudice your chance and opportunity for release if you decide to remain and help us out of this Emergency. What we are really asking is for you to defer your application for release for a further temporary period.

I read the letter with mixed feelings. By this time I had worked in the coalmines for three and a half years and this was the first time I had received thanks or appreciation for the service I had given to the Industry and to my Country. I was pleased that the Coal Board had finally recognised the work we had done as Bevin Boys to help the country in times of need. However, I was angry that it had taken so long. Since the Bevin Boy scheme started all we received was criticism from some people and comments that we were a waste of time.

Notification of release

When I received notification of my release I reported to the main office at the colliery. This was about two weeks or so before I was due to finish. At this time I asked the manager of the wages department if under the circumstances I would receive my week's holiday pay when I finished work. He told me no, that to qualify for my holiday pay the ruling was that I had to work up to the last Friday before the official summer holidays. This was if I remember right the last week in June. This meant that I would have to work another four weeks or more to qualify. The holiday period was called Trades Week. We were only allowed one week's holiday at that time. I told the Manager that I thought it very unfair as I had worked nearly a year for the money and felt that I was entitled to it. I also said that when I returned home I would be without a job and would need time to try and find one.

I was left with no other choice but to stay on at work until the holidays to qualify for my week's holiday pay. I was also upset because, unlike service men, Bevin Boys were not entitled to any grants or other benefits when de-mobbed. When I went to work next morning and told my work-mates they also thought it unfair. They said that they would be sorry to see me go. After working with them for such a long time they had got used to working with me. In the end it turned out for the best as my girl friend Lily Walton and I had been engaged about a year earlier and had arranged to get married on the September 1948 at Newtongrange.

By staying on another few weeks it would give us more time to make arrangements for the wedding. I remember while talking to the foreman a few weeks before I finished that he asked me if I would consider staying in the coalmines. I said no. I felt that working on the haulage was a dead end job and I would not consider working at the coalface. A few days later he told me that he had been making enquiries and that as there was a shortage of engineers in the mining industry at that time. Management were considering giving the opportunity to employees to go on training courses in engineering. This would only apply to those who were planning to make a career in mining.

He suggested I think it over and if I was interested to let him know and he would see what he could do for me. As I thought it over my thoughts went back to the close shaves I had. My accident, when the hutches dragged me along. The morning the foreman and I escaped the roof fall and the two occasions when I couldn't get the clip off the haulage rope and had to run to get out of the way. What I remembered most of all was the Saturday afternoon when I was on the cage going up the shaft and it suddenly dropped. I remembered how I felt at that time. I asked myself, was someone trying to tell me something. Could I risk my good luck running out? What decided me most was when I remembered that Lily, my girl friend, had agreed to come back to Corby with me after we were married.

When I saw the foreman next morning I thanked him for trying to help me but I decided not to accept his offer. If it had been made perhaps two or three years earlier it might have been different. I felt it was too late. I had made up my mind to leave the coalmines at the end of my National Service. As the time got nearer for me to leave I became unsettled. I wanted to make the most of my time left. I spent more time in Edinburgh with Lily. I also realised that I would not be able to see my Grandfather at weekends. This upset me, as I didn't know when I would see him after I returned to Corby, especially as he was getting on in years. I was also aware that I would miss the many friends I had made at work and in the village. My friends in the hostel were getting fewer every week, as they were being de-mobbed. By the time it was my time to finish most of them had gone home.

They were replaced in the hostel by miners from other parts of Scotland and also by young trainees coming into the coal industry. They too were living in the hostel. Many of them were referred to as Bevin Boys by the miners but officially they were not. I remember one in particular, his name was Arthur Higgs. He mixed well with the other lads in the hostel. I learned later that he met and married a Newtongrange girl and settled in the village.

For the next few weeks everything went on as normal. I was still kept very busy at work and didn't have much time to talk with my mates. Coal production was still on the increase in the Lady Victoria at the time and I didn't have time to think that I would soon be leaving. No one mentioned it. Suddenly it was Thursday the day before I was due to finish. When my mates were leaving at the end of the shift they said they would see me tomorrow for my last day. I can't remember saying anything. It had been so sudden.

They were looking forward to the Friday as they were going on holiday on the Saturday. When the foreman was leaving he said that he would see that I had it easy tomorrow for my last day. I returned to the hostel, showered, changed and had something to eat. I returned to my hut and sat on my bed thinking. All kind of thoughts were going through my mind. My main thought was should I go to work tomorrow? I had worked all those years down the pit and was still in one piece. Should I risk another day? I had heard over the years that some miners were reluctant to go to work on the last day before their holidays. These thoughts prayed on my mind.

It was a nice day so I thought I would go for a steady walk through the park, it was a special place to me. I had spent many happy hours there with Lily and it was where we had become engaged. After I came out of the park I went for a walk through the village. I thought about how much Newtongrange and the people meant to me and how quickly the years had passed. I had mixed feelings about leaving. Sad about leaving my friends but pleased that tomorrow was my last day working down the pit.

It still didn't help me making up my mind about going to work next day. I had a very disturbed night thinking it over. I must have gone into a sound sleep as the next thing I remember was hearing "Wakey, Wakey, First Call"! Without thinking and out of habit I got out of bed and got washed, dressed and ready for work. Then I went down to the canteen for breakfast. For the last time I collected my sandwiches, filled my flask with water and went to work without thinking about my previous doubts. I believe, what finally made up my mind was, I wanted to see my mates before I left and to say cheerio especially as they had been so helpful and looked after me all those years.

My last day as a Bevin Boy.

I was early for work. I don't know if it was intentional but I remember taking my time walking through the pit gates, collecting my tokens and lamp from the pit office for the last time. I then walked slowly up the steps, stopping when I reached the pithead. I looked at everything around me, taking it all in. I was remembering my first week there. It was as if I wanted to remember this my last day. I took my time going onto the cage and on the way down the shaft I seemed to pay more attention to the miners standing beside me. Some of them were coalface miners who worked in Trenchs section. It was the first time that I had shared the cage with them as they worked on the coalface and had further to walk. They had to leave earlier in the morning than I had to. I had a good look at the shaft on the way down. As it was summer time there were no icicles hanging from the top as there had been during the winter months.

It was like my first day all over again and it only seemed like yesterday. Where had all the years gone? While I was on the cage a couple of the miners said that they had heard that it was my last day. When the cage reached the pit bottom I followed the others off and some of them wished me good luck. I took my time to have a good look at everything around me. The miners, the hutches and the pit bottom itself. It was as if I wanted to remember everything. The years had gone so quickly and had become an important part of my life. I wanted to remember them. By the time I had reached the manhole to take off my jacket the others had long gone. When I reached the main haulage all I could see of them were lights in the distance. I thought that I would have a long lonely walk ahead of me and the haulage still hadn't started so I didn't hurry.

After a time I could see a light in the distance behind me. When it reached me it was my mate Willie Shaw. I had company for the rest of the journey and we had a good chat on the way. I was pleased the way things turned out. He was with me on my first day and now on my last. When we reached the landing at where Bill Currie works, he was there. He always reported early and his first words were "you're early, couldn't you sleep?" I had a few minutes with him before going in to Whitehill Mine where I would be taking over my duties for the last time.

There were no empty hutches waiting and no full ones ready to come out, I had cleared them all the day before. I had time to have a good chat with Bob Scott. After a time the foreman Dave Young arrived. He said he was pleased to see me as he wasn't sure if I would come in on my last day. I told him that I wanted to see everyone before I left to say cheerio. He told me that I would have the whole of the shift to do that. He had arranged for someone to do my job for the rest of the shift. I made the best of the time and visited all my friends and thanked them for all the help they had given me. I shook Davy Young's hand for the last time and thanked him for the help and support he gave me since my first day. I must admit I was happy that this was my last day down the pit but felt a bit sad, knowing that I might not see my friends again. I did see some of them at times when I visited Newtongrange in later years.

At the end of the shift I joined the others. There were five or six of us and we walked to the pit bottom together. For the last time, I collected my jacket from the manhole slowly making my way towards the cage. I had a good look around me. I was quiet on the way up the shaft. Soon we arrived at the pithead and made our way to the pit office and handed in our lamps and tokens. At the pit gates I looked back before shaking everyone by the hand and thanking them once more, they wished me luck.

From there I made my way across to the wages department to collect my wages and the various documents I would require to start another job in Corby. I was told they weren't ready and would I call back later. I was then asked if I had been to work that day. I was upset by this time and said that they could see that I have. Perhaps they didn't want to make up my wages until they were sure I been to work. I called back when I had been washed, changed and had something to eat. By that time everything was ready for me to collect. I decided to wait until the Saturday before leaving the hostel.

I would like to have waited for a few more days especially as it was a holiday but I had to get back home to Corby. I needed to find a job as soon as possible and every day counted. On the Saturday Lily and I spent the day in Edinburgh. When we returned to Newtongrange I spent some time with her family before returning to the hostel, to get packed and to check out of the hostel for the last time. I then said goodbye to the few mates that were left as most of the Bevin Boys I had known since I arrived had been released and gone home by this time. I caught the bus to Edinburgh, as I had to be at Waverley Station to catch the train about 10 p.m. for Corby.

Going home to Corby

The train to London always passed over the viaduct at the outskirts of Newtongrange. As I had always done in the past I went into the corridor of the train to look down at Newtongrange. From where I was standing it seemed that I was looking into a valley. I wondered if Lily was watching the train as it passed that night, as she would often do when I was going to Corby on holiday. When I went back to my seat in the carriage lots of things went through my mind. I remember how upset I was when called up to work in the coalmines and here I was upset because I was going home. Had I made the right decision?

Only time would tell. I know that I would not have missed the experience of working in the pits, living in the mining community and meeting such wonderful people.

I was feeling sad for many reasons. I was leaving a village that had been my home for nearly four years. This was twice as long as I had lived in Corby and where I had made many good friends. I then remembered I would be returning to Newtongrange in a few weeks time to get married and meet up with some friends again. After a time I went to sleep only waking up when passengers were getting off and on the train. When I arrived in Corby it was about 7.00a.m on the Sunday morning. My family were pleased to see me. It had been a few months since I had been home and we had lots to talk about.

Starting back to work

Early on the Monday morning I went down to Stewarts & Lloyds to look for a job. I reported to the Main Office and explained that I had been de-mobbed as a Bevin Boy and was looking for work. The girl in the office got out my records from my previous job. She told me that the Tube Mill where I worked before had been dismantled. I was pleased, as I didn't want to go back there. I was told that as I was considered a new start I would have to join a labouring gang. I started work on the Tuesday morning mixing concrete. After a week I was given a job as a fitter's mate in the Blower House covering for someone who was on holiday. After two weeks my foreman said he was pleased with my work and asked me if I would be interested in a job in the General Stores Spares Department. I accepted his offer and felt better knowing that I would have a steady job when I returned to Corby after the wedding.

Returning to Newtongrange

I was looking forward to returning to Newtongrange to make the final arrangements for the wedding but Lily and her mother had arranged everything. I had nothing to worry about. It was a happy day for me when Lily and I were married in the Church of Scotland on the 8th September. 1948. The Church is directly across the road from where Lily lived with her family at the bottom of Sixth Street. A few days later Lily returned with me to Corby. We have lived there ever since. A Happy Ending to my years as a Bevin Boy and a New Beginning.

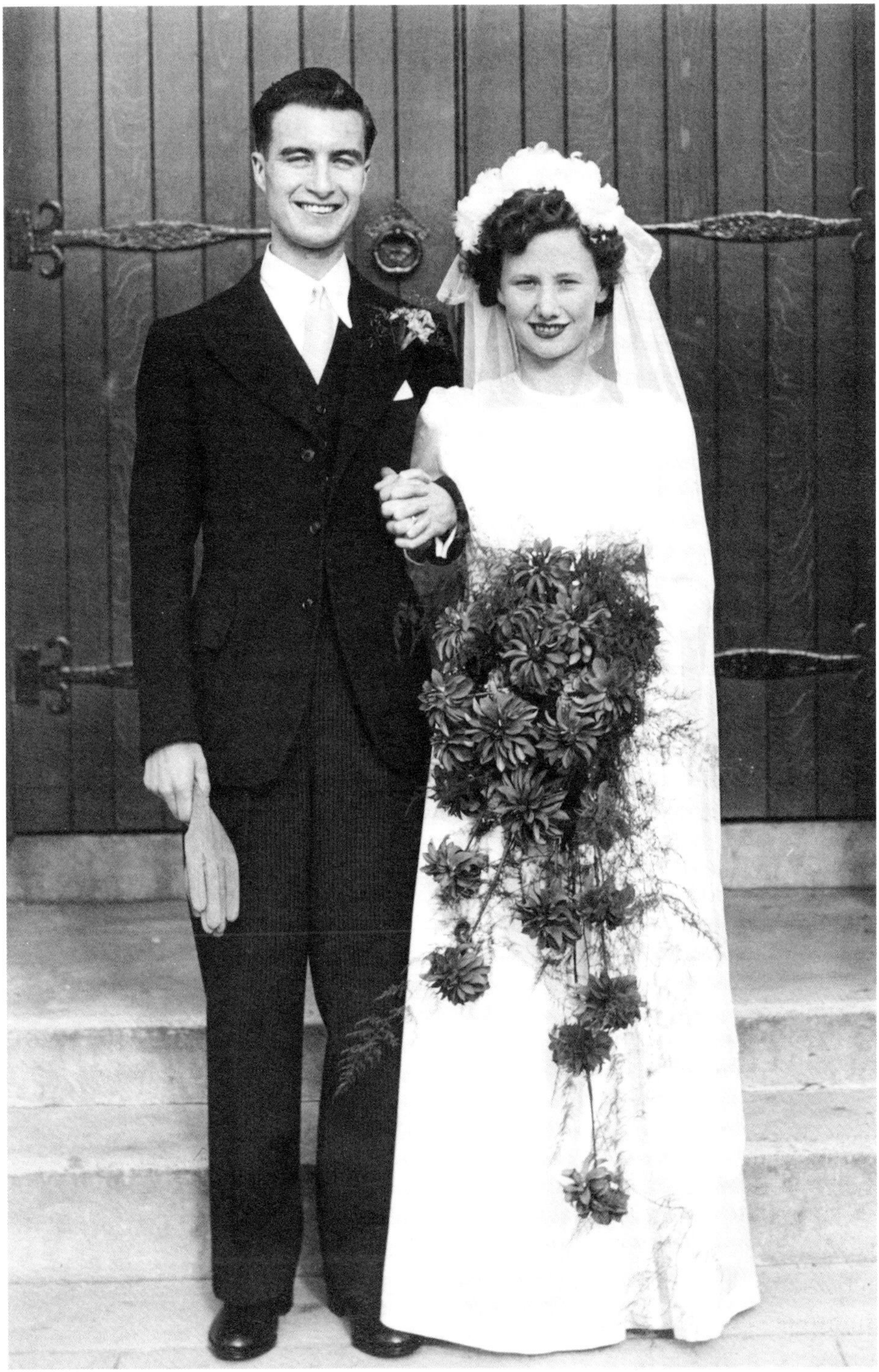

Visit to The Lady Victoria Scottish Mining Museum (2000)

I would like to finish my story by telling you about a special event that took place more than 50 years later after I was released from the coalmines. As a member of The Bevin Boy's Association, I was one of about fifty Bevin Boys and their wives who attended a Millennium Special Reunion at the University of Edinburgh in April 2000.

We visited many of the attractions in Edinburgh including The Castle and Princes Street. We also visited the Former Royal Yacht 'Britannia'. The special event for me was a visit to The Lady Victoria, which had now become The Scottish Mining Museum. I was happy to be joined with my friends from the Association to let them see where I worked as a Bevin Boy. It brought back so many memories.
Some of my friends mentioned how fortunate I was to be able to visit the pit where I had worked as theirs had been flattened years earlier. I think what I impressed them most was that they could see from a distance the two large wheels above the winding engine.

As a 'Friend' of The Mining Museum I was delighted to attend a Presentation by Robert Garret on behalf of 'The Friends of the Museum'. A wooden bench was presented to the Bevin Boys in recognition of their service to the coal industry at a time when it was needed. The bench was placed in the entrance to the Museum to rest the weary legs of visitors as there is so much to see.

Bevin Boys Re-Union
Lady Victoria 2000

PRESENTATION OF SEAT BY THE FRIENDS OF THE SCOTTISH MINING MUSEUM TO THE BEVIN BOYS

Warwick Taylor (standing)
Robert Garret (sitting)

Don Mocket (standing
George Ralston (sitting)

SCOTTISH MINING MUSEUM.

The Scottish Mining Museum at the Lady Victoria Colliery, Newtongrange. The museum is an independent charity working to preserve the memory of this once great industry. Visitors can tour the massive colliery buildings and see the great winding engine, displays of mining equipment and a mock-up of a modern coal face. An audio-visual show and permanent changing exhibition present a history of mining life.

The museum is ten miles south of Edinburgh on the A7 road.

For opening times and further information, contact. Telephone; 0131 663 7519.